THE GREAT AWAKENING

Volume - IV

A series of superbly informative and prophetic messages,
downloaded and transcribed originally as newsletters by

Sister Thedra

These precious messages are reprinted herein.

ISBN: 978-1-7363418-0-3

Contents

Mission Statement

Give the truth to the world. Let it be received where it will. Many will read the messages. Some will accept the truth, others will read through curiosity, a few will ridicule. Yet to all is the truth given, and to all remains the power of choice.

The hope of the world in these times is in spiritualizing all forms of activity---promoting understanding through love and service. These must be the watchwords if the world is to come into lasting peace. We are trying to influence a world that is going astray and could cause undreamed of suffering. We are trying to overcome the thought of materialists and to bring a spiritual outlook into the earthly life. We need the help of all on earth who can think in spiritual terms. The great battle to be fought now is between the spiritual and the material, between idealism and carnalism. You can help by spreading the word---we are asking that you help because the battle may be long and the victory far away.

Halls of Light is not allied with any sect, denomination, political entity, organization, neither endorses nor opposes any cause. There are no dues for membership. Halls of Light is self-supporting through its own voluntary contributions. Halls of Light has but one purpose: to help through encouragement and understanding...

To contact the publishers or to obtain copies of our other books, please contact us at email: goldtown11@gmail.com

Esu Jesus Sananda

This reproduction is from an actual photograph taken on June 1st, 1961, in Chichen Itza, Yucatan, by one of thirty archaeologists working in the area at the time. Sananda appeared in visible, tangible body and permitted His photograph to be taken.

THE TEMPLE OF SANANDA & SANAT KUMARA

Christmas - 1974

Sori Sori --Be ye as Mine hand made manifest unto them - say unto them as I would, that there shall be peace when they have given unto Me their hearts, their hands, their whole self - they shall then know peace, or it shall be established within them.

They shall have no hatred or animosity within them, for it is the way of the transgressor to be tormented by the hatred and hypocrisy - while the initiate finds peace within himself, for he is given unto peace.

Therefore I say unto them which cry: "Peace - Peace – Peace": First establish it within thine own self, and let others profit thereby. While I say unto <u>ALL</u>: "PEACE" - they have not partaken of Mine Peace, for they know Me not.

They have found not peace within their churches - their temples - their places of learning; neither have they turned into their Source for Peace. They have been found in the "Places of worship" crying long and loud for so-called "peace", yet it hast availed them naught, for they have looked unto man - they have sought out their "Wise men" and consulted their oracles, and for that do I see them as ones defeated/confused - running hither and yon as ones bewildered - while I stand before them, crying out: "Come unto Me and mow ye Peace as I know, for I am the Lord of Hosts, sent of Mine Father that there be Peace established within them. I see them as bound in darkness, knowing not that I am come, even as the thief in the night.

I have said: "Wait ye no more! come ye out from among them and follow where I lead thee, that ye might go where I go".

So be it that I am come to deliver out them which seek Me out - which hunger for the Light which I AM.

Fashion no gods for thyself; ask not of man - make ye no images of Me, for I am the Lord thy God! I am not bound by thine imaginings - thine preconceived ideas or opinions of Me. I am the Risen Lord, the Lord of Lords, come that ye might know the true from the false - and I say there are false gods which would mislead the unwise - the mistaken - the ones bound by the father of lies, for he carefully lays his traps to mislead and misguide them which are unaware of his schemes. I say his nefarious schemes have fallen on the fertile soil of them which seek signs and wonders - them which lay themself at his feet and ask for miracles; for he can and does show them marvels and signs - yet wherein has he freed them from bondage? He holds them bound in the places wherein they do languish, and cry out for Mine assistance. These are the ones which have followed him into the pit wherein he forsakes them - for he cares not for them after they have served his purpose.

I say he, the father of lies forsakes them and leaves them to languish in the pit. So be it ye shall do well to turn from him ere it is too late. I am thoughtful of thee, even in the time of thine torment and anguish. I say unto thee which follow me, I am mindful of thee - even into the pit I reach out in Love and Mercy that they be delivered. So be it wise to hear ye Me, that ye be spared the fate of the traitors - for there are none so sad.

Let it be well with thee when that hour comes that ye are called to go forth into the place of abode wherein ye shall be within thine new environment. I say the day swiftly approaches when thy name shall be called, and ye shall answer - let it be well with thee. Let it not be said, thou hast not heard Me, for I have called out unto thee: "Arise! Come ye out and be ye made whole".

I give Mine Peace unto all which hear Mine Voice and respond unto it. So let it be for all which have ears to hear, and a will to go where I go, for

I Am the Lord thy God

Recorded by Sister Thedra

October 11, 1975

Sanat Kumara speaking:

You have chosen to associate yourself with ASSK and have become a student of the teachings offered thereby. Know that this is no earthly club or institution but is the manifest and outward expression of the inner school -- the Association being founded on the highest of principles.

To be associated in this regard means a certain responsibility for one's conduct and demeanor that will enhance, rather than deter, the work going on. For this Temple is a vital link in the plan now going into effect on planet Earth, and everyone associated with the Gate House must come to realize the import of the work being done there.

Take the opportunity, when it presents itself, to impress upon those brothers and sisters closely associated with the Gate House, the far-reaching importance of the work being done there. Nothing must interfere; all must be ever aware that the Father's business is of primary importance; all else must become secondary.

Sister Thedra is well aware of this. The burden upon her weighs heavily, for she has taken the responsibility for being the Coordinator -- the Priestess of the Temple. Her devotion and purpose is single -- her inner knowledge vast -- for she knows without a doubt the part she has chosen, and she is playing it well. Her burden would be eased if others begin to realize the seriousness of the work and the import of ASSK from a higher vantage point.

We of the Grand Council play an active part in the activities at the Gate House, and work hand in hand with our brothers there in flesh bodies, that the work expand and grow until it reaches the far corners of the Earth. Quietly do we go about our business, and in a calm and purposeful attitude.

As the Plan unfolds bit by bit, the activities of ASSK will mold themselves accordingly. Direction and guidance will be ever at hand.

Remember thy purpose -- obey the Law -- and perform thy new work with diligence and joy. We bless you and welcome you.

I am thy elder brother,

Sanat Kumara

Recorded by Margot

4

Nov. 13, 1975

Sananda speaking:

Sori Sori -- Heed ye well the words of My Beloved Priestess, for in her hands have I placed My authority. She has given herself as one to be used by Me for the service of mankind. I speak through her; she is My mouthpiece; she is My voice made manifest.

In many ways has she offered herself to be used - and she has proven herself to be trustworthy and dependable. For this reason she will be given much greater responsibility, for in the doing on her present work, she has proven herself well - she has prepared herself for that which lies ahead.

In this wise is she an example for you to follow - she has allowed nothing to block the passage-way for communication between us. Many obstacles, too large for her to move alone have appeared in her path - but her faith has not wavered one iota; neither has she become side-tracked in the effort to remove it; forgetting the matter at hand, she has put first and foremost the work to be done - and so she has received countless help in removing the obstacles.

Among men she is little recognized, and has withstood much adversity, mockery, mud-slinging for My sake. Neither has this removed her from her chosen path for even one brief moment.

Wise is he who observes her work, and learns from her speaking and writing, for in this wise does he learn from Me.

I do not come to flatter, but to awaken My children unto the obvious - that which they see darkly, and do not recognize.

Man's Foolishness vs Peace

Sori Sori - We come unto thee out the firmaments, we give unto thee of Ourself that the whole be made perfect - for perfect it was, and perfect shall it be. Yet man hast dunged unto the waters which hast been unto him the Life Force; he hast destroyed that which wast given unto him as his fortune that he be comforted and protected. The way of man is indeed pitiful; it is said he is not self-sufficient; he has not proven himself sufficient, neither responsible for his own well-being.

Therefore I say unto him, he shall bestir himself and arise from out his self-made mire and come unto Me as one, and there shall be peace and unity among men.

From out the chaos shall he bring peace when he, man, finds that he is responsible for his own torment - the hell he hast created for himself.

Contracts/pacts hast he made; peace treaties by the score he hast made, while he hast not found peace within himself; there shall be no peace until he creates it within himself!

Now the part I would give unto thee at this hour, is the preparation of a new part. Ye shall give unto them this Word, and it shall be unto them that which is needful, and it shall be unto then great wisdom if they but learn from it - when they learn the folly of giving unto themself credit for being wise. They have not been wise in the dealing with their fellow man; they have not found that they have not the wisdom to deal out Justice one unto the other; they sit in judgment and call themself "wise" in their conceit.

I say, behold ye O man in thine own conceit and in thine own foolishness.

When thou hast turned unto thine Source of Being, and asked for the Truth of all things, ye shall become the better able to deal out Justice, and peace shall be established within thee.

There shall be no peace until thou hast learned well thy lessons. "Love ye one another"; forget not that ye have been warned that the time is NOW come to assess thy own self; of all thine inmost parts; that which thou hast hidden away in the dark recesses of thine inmost part/ in thine closet.

Bring forth that which lies buried therein and assess it - forgetting not that ye alone are responsible for the hidden part of thy fortune which now comes to the surface to torment thee.

Search out that which torments thee and put it from thee; forgive thine own self thy foolishness and forgetfulness; thine lethargy. Be alert and aright thineself; turn unto the Light and many things shall be shown unto thee.

Pray for assistance and it shall not be denied. So be it that I have spoken unto ALL alike, and I stand ready to extend Mine hand unto each one which turns unto me with a contrite heart and a will to learn of Me.

I shall do Mine part - let it be so with thee, and all shall be well with thee - so be it Amen, and Amen. I am the Lord thy God Sent that there be Light in the world of men. So let it be and Selah.

Recorded by Sister Thedra

November 2, 1975

Ye Are Not Alone - The Power of The Word

Sarah speaking: - Beloved of my being: Be ye blest of me and by me for I come unto thee that ye may be blest. I say unto thee: It is now come when great shall be thy revelations. I say that great things shall be revealed unto thee, and it is so. So be it.

I come that they may have Light; that all men might have Light. So be it and Selah. I speak unto thee these words that they may have them, and that they might learn of me, and that they might be brought out of bondage. Such is my love for them.

I say that they are not alone in their little world which they create for themself. I say: They are not alone upon the tiny "Red Star" - "Terra". They are not alone in their hiding places, for I say unto them, there is no hiding place! for they are not alone. I say there are no secrets - only their unknowing, which is the result of having their memory blanked from them.

I say: When their memory was blanked from them, they went into darkness, and they lost the power of the "WORD" which was God, and which IS GOD. I say: They are not enlightened in their knowing, they are as ones groping in darkness.

They have the memory stored in the secret closet wherein they file all their deeds, all their opinions, all their guilt, all their sorrows; and these they lock safely within their own secret place wherein they go in the hours of their sleep, and recount their experiences one by one, as their rosaries.

And they cherish the memory of that which has given unto them pleasure of the animal senses - animal nature, and they are as ones bound unto these things which have given unto them pleasure and sorrow, until they free themself from the animal nature - in the senses, which are of the animal kingdom.

Such is the law. I say: Ye are as one bound by these senses, until ye have purified thy own self of every vestige of the animal senses, the anger passions of the animal, and the grossness which belongs unto the animal kingdom.

I say: Ye shall go into thy secret place and bring out all that which ye have buried therein, and examine it, remember it for that which it is. Forgive thyself for thy foolishness, and thy unknowing. Unlock thy "leg irons" and turn from them, and walk away from them as one unbound, as a free man. I say unto thee it is that simple. I say, ye alone can unlock thy leg irons.

We of the Golden Helmeted Ones can but show the way; We can but point out the pitfalls, and lead thee up and direct thee. Yet I say: Ye shall walk in the way set before thee.

I say: Ye shall be as ones which have a mind to learn, and the will, and One shall be sent unto thee which shall bring thee out of the place wherein ye are, and ye shall find a place prepared for thee, wherein ye may dwell thruout all eternity, in freedom and in Light and Love which is, which was and ever shall be, worlds without end. So be it and Selah. I am thy Mother Eternal, Sarah.

Recorded by Sister Thedra

Stephani

"The Initiates Walk Among Us"

Beloved of My Being: Be ye as one blest of me and by me. I come unto thee that they might have this my Word.

I say unto them which are yet within the world of men, that when it is come that they are delivered up, they shall be as ones wise; they shall be as ones liberated, and they shall be as ones which have received their sonship of God the Father.

I say: Many of the Sons of God walk among thee, free from any and all limitation. Yet they appear even as ye, for they move in silence - they flaunt not their wisdom nor their learning before man. They speak wisely and prudently. They know when to speak, and poised are they; and they are at peace, for they know themself for that which they are.

They have no false gods, neither do they bow down unto any man, for they fear no man, no thing. They carry within their hand the "Rod of Power", they carry no weapons, only the Sword of Truth - the two-edged sword, and they are as ones prepared for any occasion.

I speak unto thee from out the monitor ship, the XTX, and upon which are many which are being prepared to go forth as ones which shall walk among thee as emissaries, and they shall find thee, that is, (they shall find) the ones which are prepared, and which are found trustworthy and worth the effort. I say: The ones which have a will to serve unto the end - which are prepared to endure all things according to the law.

And the ones which are obedient unto the law shall be found and given assistance, and they shall be as ones which are the servants, and they shall serve in the great and Divine Plan. I say that they shall serve the plan which is designed to deliver all mankind from bondage forever.

Now I speak unto them which have a will to serve: Be ye alert, and give unto the Father credit for thy Being, and unto thy Benefactors credit for thy well being, and they shall give unto thee a hand. So be it and Selah.

I am Stephani

Recorded by Sister Thedra

There Shall Be Great Suffering

Sanat Kumara speaking:- Be ye blest of my presence and of my being - I come that ye may be blest. I give unto thee my love and of my time that ye might be blest. I speak unto thee this day, as One which has gone before thee, that he might find thy way. I speak unto thee that ye might find thy way, yet ye shall be as ones responsible for thy own preparation, and ye shall walk in the way set before thee.

11

I say: The law is clearly stated, and ye shall apply thyself; in all thy ways ye shall remember that which has been given unto thee. I say: Ye shall profit thereby. And give nothing unto them which they can use against thee; I say: Ye shall keep for thyself that which is given unto thee, and that which is given unto thee for them, give unto them, and they shall receive it in the name of the Father, Son and Holy Ghost, amen and Selah. I say: Ye shall say unto them as I would say, that they shall bear witness of these my words, and they shall remember them, for it is given unto me to see and to know that which is, that which shall be, and that which has been.

It is now come when there shall be mighty winds, and there shall be great suffering and much sorrow. And there shall be many homeless and fraught with fear and disease.

And ye shall be as ones which have upon thy shoulders great responsibility, for ye shall be as ones prepared to bring comfort and peace wherein there is no comfort and no peace. I say: Ye shall prepare thyself for that which shall be given unto thee to do. So be it and Selah. I say: Ye shall prepare thyself for thy part, and when this is done We thy Sibors shall do our part.

I say unto them which are yet in the sleeper's realm, that they shall alert themself, and they shall awaken and be up and about the Father's business. I say ye have slept overtime; too I say, that great is the work which is accomplished while ye have slept. While ye have slept, many have walked thy highways and thy byways, which have within their hand the power to deliver thee up; yet ye have not recognized them, nor have ye asked that ye know them. Ye are bound by thy own opinions and by thy dogmas; I say ye are bound by thy own opinions and by thy own dogmas. Ye shall be as ones free from all opinions, from all dogma. Ye shall stand as one free from all bondage forever.

I say: Ye shall ask of God the Father for LIGHT and for thy freedom - such shall profit thee. So be it and Selah.

I am thy older brother, Sanat Kumara

Recorded by Sister Thedra

Berea

"Be Ye Single of Eye"

Berea speaking:- Beloved of my Being: Be ye as my hand unto them and say unto them as I would say that there are many among them which are prepared to give unto them the Water of Life. And they walk among thee. Ye shall prepare thyself and give unto thy preparation the proper attention and ye shall be glad. For it is now come when great shall be thy trials and temptations. Ye shall be alert, and ye shall be as ones which have thy eye single, and thy heart fixed upon thy goal.

I say ye shall not divide thyself - ye shall be as <u>one</u> - ye shall be as "one undivided". It is said that ye have divided thy time, spent thy energy in frivolity, and ye have gone the long way to serve the forces of darkness. Ye have been unto thyself traitor; ye are as yet bound by the forces of darkness. I say the dragon is not of mind to release thee - he shall fight unto the last to hold thee fast. So be it ye shall will thy freedom; alert thyself and he shall not pursue thee. I say, he shall not hold thee against thy will.

13

Be ye blest of them which are sent that ye might have thy freedom. So be it that it shall profit thee to reach out and accept that which We offer unto thee, in the name of the Most High Living God. So be it and Selah.

I say unto thee: We are of the Father sent, and we give unto thee as He gives unto us for thee. So be it and Selah.

I come that ye may have the greater part - such is my love for thee. I join my beloved Sanat Kumara in this endeavor, that the fullness of the plan might be realized, and that ye might be part of it. I say that the ones which do awaken and alert themself shall sit in council with us as part of the great and Divine Plan. So be it and Selah.

I say that they which are the sleepers shall sleep on. So be it and Selah. I speak unto thee from out the fullness of my heart, and I know whereof I speak. So be it and Selah. I am with thee and ye have but to accept Me - My Love - My hand, and I shall make known unto thee many wonderful things. So be it and Selah.

I am thy older sister - thy Sibor, Berea

Recorded by Sister Thedra of the Emerald Cross

- The Signs - The End of the age -

Berea speaking:- Be ye blest of my boing, and say unto them as I would say, that it is now come when they shall be as ones prepared. For when they shall see the great and glorious signs which shall be manifest from the realms of Light; and when they shall see the great

14

darkness descend upon the earth; and when they shall see prophecy fulfilled; they shall see and know that the end of the age is come.

I say: They shall see the handwriting upon the wall, and they shall read while they run.

I say. These are great signs, and ye shall be as ones which have the mind to read, and to know the meaning thereof.

Say I unto thee: Be ye of a mind to learn, and great things shall be revealed unto thee. I say: The signs of the times are written within the sky, within the stones; they are marked, and the waters give up their secrets.

I say that the Earth shall give up her secrets; she shall be as an open book; she shall be relieved of all her spoils - of her burden, for she has held her secrets jealously, and she shall be glad for her freedom. So be it she shall be freed from her bondage - forever free, for she shall pass out of her present port into clear waters, wherein she shall rest - wherein she shall have peace and rest, wherein she shall be prepared to receive the Sons of God which shall inherit the NEW EARTH. I say they shall inherit the NEW EARTH. So be it and Selah. I say the Earth shall be cleansed and renewed - so be it her inheritance. So be it and Selah.

I speak unto them which are as ones yet in darkness, and I say: Ye shall come to know that which is fortuned unto thee; ye shall awaken, and ye shall be as ones wise to alert thyself, for it is now come when the Earth shall no longer give unto the IDOLATORS, and into the sleepers comfort - she shall cast them off her back. So be it ye shall be put into a place which has been prepared for thee.

I say: Be ye as ones alert! and HEAR ME! and remember these my words, and mark them well, for they shall stand thee in good stead.

Be ye as ones which have a WILL to HEAR.

I am come that ye may be prepared for the greater part, which is thy own Godhood. So be it and Selah.

I am Berea

Recorded by Sister Thedra of the Emerald Cross

"I See Them"

Berea speaking: - Beloved of my Being: Be ye as my hand made manifest unto them, and say unto them as I would say, that there are ones which walk among them, which are prepared to give unto them the Waters of Life.

I say that there is One which is come, which has within his hand the power to give unto thee the Crystal Goblet. And ye have but to purify thyself, and he shall find thee, and he shall seek thee out when the hour strikes, and ye shall be glad for thy effort. I say: Ye shall be glad for thy effort - such is my word unto thee.

Be ye blest this day, and give unto them this my word, and ye shall be as my hand and as my voice, for I say unto them: It is now come when many shall walk among us as ones qualified to lift them up. And they shall be alert and walk with their head high, and they shall be as ones which have upon their head a crown, and they shall walk which way it tilts not. So be it it shall be becoming unto them.

I say they shall walk in the way set before them; they shall turn not to the left nor to the right.

I say: They shall be as ones on whose shoulders rests the responsibility of their own salvation.

I speak unto them out of the fullness of time - I see and know. I see them as ones filled with longing - with care - with fear. I see them running to and fro - I see them going and coming. I see them as ones bowed down with grief and despair. I see them as ones bound hand and foot, knowing not by what they are bound.

I see them weary of the load which they have fortuned unto themself. I see them as ones looking for a magical formula, which shall be unto them a poultice. I see them filled with hatred, filled with shame.

I see them which give unto thee the bitter cup. I see them which withhold their hearts and their service. I see them which are as the babblers, and their tongues are as the asp's.

I see them as one's unbridled; they run riot; their emotions know no bounds; they are as the ones untrained, unlearned; they are as ones yet in darkness; they are as ones undisciplined; they are as children - little children - unlearned in the ways of the initiate.

I say: They have not as yet begin their work, and they are as ones which think themself wise. So be it and Selah. I speak into them frankly and fearlessly; I say that which is given into me to say, and no man shall set his hand unto my mouth, for I come that they may awaken, and I give not my pearls without price. I say I give not my pearls unto babes who know not their worth. I speak of the unlearned, and of the ones which "think" themself wise.

I say unto them which are within the gate, that there are none so foolish as the one which thinks himself wise, and none so sad as - the one which betrays himself.

I speak unto them which serve the Father day and night; I speak unto the ones which are alert, and which are of a mind to walk in the way set before them; that thy reward shall be great - thy service rewarded - thy heart shall be filled with joy and thanksgiving. Ye shall remember that which is said - ye shall apply thyself wholeheartedly - ye shall hold fast unto the law.

Ye shall not weary in that which is good.

Ye shall not join them in their foolishness.

Ye shall see them for that which they are - and not for their deeds.

Ye shall not wait for their opinion and their approval - ye shall go straitway upon thy appointed course.

Ye shall ask of the Father and he shall answer thee - ye shall have no gods before thee.

Ye shall be as his foot, and as his hand made manifest upon the Earth.

Ye shall walk with him, and talk with him, and ye shall know as he knows - so be it thy inheritance. I say he, the Father is not mocked, neither is he deceived. He is not deceived - he is not mocked.

I say: He which is so foolish as to try to mimic him, or to give unto him the lie, is the greatest of fools - poor in spirit are they.

I say: Ye shall be blest of me this day. Ye have received me this day, in the name of the Father, Son and Holy Ghost. So be it I shall remember thee.

I am Berea

Recorded by Sister Thedra of the Emerald Cross

Thou Shall - Thou Shall Not

Berea speaking:- Beloved of my being: Be ye blest this day of me and by me. I come that ye may be blest. So be it and Selah. Be ye as one prepared for the greater part.

I say: Ye shall be as one on whose shoulders rests great responsibility, for ye shall go out from the place wherein ye are as one prepared. I say: Ye shall go out from the place wherein ye are as one prepared. So be it and Selah.

Be ye as my hand made manifest unto them which shall read these words, and they shall bear witness of that which I say; they shall remember these words, and they shall not desecrate them.

Be as ones which have a mind to comprehend these things which I say unto thee, and comprehension shall be given unto thee. Ye shall

NOW be as ones willing to follow in the footsteps of the WAYSHOHER;

Ye shall walk in the way He sets before thee,

Ye shall prepare thyself,

Ye shall do that which He commands of thee,

Ye shall be as ones brot out from among them, (the world)

Ye shall be no part of their foolishness,

Ye shall not join in the foolish parts which they fortune unto themself,

Ye shall be as a thing apart,

Ye shall dare to be different from "them",

Ye shall stand as the ROCK, and ye shall be unmoved,

Ye shall hold steadfast unto RIGHTEOUSNESS.

Ye shall plant thy feet on the solid rock, hold thy head high, and KNOW I AM GOD; THE SON OF GOD I AM, and nothing shall touch thee. So be it and Selah.

I come unto thee that this may be given unto thee, and they shall have it at the earliest time possible. So be it and Selah. I am with thee unto the end. I am thy Older Sister and Sibor, Berea.

Recorded by Sister Thedra of the Emerald Cross

Nothing Shall Be Added To

Beloved of my Being: I speak with thee this day that they might know me; I come unto thee that they may know me.

I say unto them that there are many which walk among them as man, which would give unto them the Water of LIFE, and I say unto them: They shall be as ones prepared to receive of him, for they walk among thee, and they seek out them which are prepared; and they shall be the hand of the Father; they shall put out their hand, and it shall be filled - so be it the law, as ye are prepared so shall ye receive.

Ye shall be about thy preparation, for none other shall be responsible for thee. So be it and Selah.

I say unto thee that which is given unto me to say of the Father, for I speak, that which he wills that I say - I speak as he would speak.

Be ye as one which has the mind to hear, and the will to do. Be ye as one prepared for the NEW DAY, when all things shall be made NEW - when the OLD shall pass away, and the SONS of GOD shall inherit the NEW EARTH, and the NEW HEAVENS.

Be ye as one responsible for thy own preparation. I say the law is clearly written within these times - and that which has been recorded within this temple, at this Altar is true - TRUTH! untampered with. I say it is that which has been spoken from out the realms of Light, and by the enlightened ones.

I say: NOT ONE WORD shall be misplaced, or taken away; I say nothing shall be added to.

I say that the recorder of these scripts has been, and is TRUE unto herself, and I say, she has OBEYED every commandment. And too I say, she shall not want - she shall be rewarded as a faithful servant. This is my word unto thee. So be it and Selah.

NOW I say unto thee, which I call the faithful servant: Ye shall make a copy of this, and send it into the ones referred to as Unit No. 3, and they shall bear witness of these my words.

I sign myself, Berean

Recorded by Sister Thedra of the Emerald Cross

Peace and Poise

Beloved of My Being: Be ye blest of My presence and of My being. I come that you may be blest - so be it and Selah. I speak unto thee for the good of all mankind - so let it be. Be ye as My hand made manifest unto them which are of a mind to hear that which I say unto them.

I say unto them, that when it is come that they are called to "COME OUT FROM AMONG THEM", that it is a great plan which has been given unto us thy Benefactors, which see and know the whole Plan.

Yet I say that when we give unto thee that which ye know not, ye are ofttimes fearful and disobedient - ye are fearful of being deceived for the ones which would misuse thee and deceive thee, use many guises and many ruses. I say they will go to the end to distract and confuse thee - so be ye as wise as the serpent and firm as the rock.

Be ye of a mind to give unto the Father thy whole heart, thy hand and thy will, and ask of HIM thy freedom; and I say unto thee: NOTHING shall come nigh unto thee which is of darkness.

Let not thy fears consume thee; be ye not fearful, for I say unto thee: Ye shall be brot out of bondage. So be it and Selah.

I come that ye may be brot out, and I am glad this day is come, when ye might know the plan which has been brot forth. I say: The plan is designed for this day, when ye may return unto thy Source without tasting of death - such is the plan.

Now I would say unto thee one word which shall stand thee four square: Be ye at PEACE and POISE, and let nothing be unto thee a thorn in thy foot. I say ye shall walk with surety at all times ye shall not fall, neither shall ye falter. So be it ye shall not be left alone, nor shall ye perish! I say, be ye at PEACE and POISE.

Blest shall ye be - I am come that ye might have peace. So be it and Selah.

Be ye as one which has my hand upon thee and I shall bless thee. So be it and Selah.

I am thy older Brother and thy Sibor, Sananda

Recorded by sister Thédra of the Emerald Cross

Praise Him - Sori Sori

Sori Sori -- Behold I am come; I enter within thy temple - I come as thy guest. I bless thee - I speak unto thee in accent sweet; I prepare thee for the great communion of the Sons of God. I bring unto thee sweet fragrance - I come with the sword of TRUTH. I bring the torch of freedom - I place it within thy hand. I speak unto thee that which the Father wills.

I give unto thee the key unto the KINGDOM OF GLORY, and the KING shall enter within the time which is near. Praise the Father Mother God. Lift up thine eyes - behold all things made new. I come that all things may be made new. So be it and Selah.

Be ye as one made whole -

Praise ye O my soul -

Lift up thine eyes unto the heavens -

Bow down unto no man -

Hold high thine head -

Sing ye the PRAISE of Father Mother God, which has given unto thee being.

Bless them which spitefully use thee.

Give unto thyself credit for being a Son of God the Father.

Bless thee O my soul - Be ye eternally blest -

Call and ye shall be heard -

I shall serve thee diligently.

O my child, PRAISE ye this day, IT IS COME! IT IS COME!

I say unto thee: IT IS COME! Give unto the Father all the credit and the Glory.

Praise ye the name of SOLEN AUM SOLEN - for I say unto thee: He has given unto thee being, and unto Him all the PRAISE AND THE GLORY.

SING, YE LANDS OF THE EARTH!

HEAR ME, YE PEOPLE OF THE EARTH!

IT IS COME, when the waters shall be divided,

And the hills shall be leveled,

And the rains shall come,

And the winds shall blow,

And families shall be divided,

And fire and water shall mix,

And the torrents shall run uphill,

And the winds shall fan the fires,

And great destruction shall come upon the Earth.

Yet I say unto thee: ALL THESE THINGS are but the beginning of the GLORIOUS NEW DAWN!

Be at PEACE, and give thanks that it is come!

I say that they which are privileged to partake of this time - this day - this age, are as ones blest forever. So be it and Selah.

Would ye not PROFIT for thy own sake?

I say: Be ye as one blessed, for great shall be thy reward.

HOLY is HIS name - which ye shall remember - and speak.

PRAISE ye the name of SOLEN AUM SOLEN, and keep it ever within thine heart - keep it holy and immaculate. Fear not, and walk ye with SURETY. Place thine hand in HIS - yield not unto temptation, and ye shall be delivered up.

Praise ye all the days of thy LIFE, and be ye at PEACE. Bring the labor of thy hands unto the Altar of the Most High LIVING GOD, and great shall be thy reward.

Blest shall ye be.

Bring thyself as a living sacrifice unto the Altar, and it shall be acceptable unto HIM the KING of GLORY, and ye shall abide with HIM forever more.

Be ye at PEACE and POISE.

Blest be ye my child -

I am with thee unto the end -

I am known as One without end - without beginning.

I AM the ALPHA and the OMEGA -

I know myself to BE - so AM I. So be it - Selah.

Sori Sori

Recorded by Sister Thedra of the Emerald Cross

Sananda

"Be Ye Responsible"

Beloved of My Being:- I come unto thee this day that ye may be blest - so be it and Selah. I say ye shall be blest, and I give unto thee this word for them, that they too might be blest.

Be ye as ones prepared for the day which is now come, and ye shall be as ones which have my hand upon thee, and I shall bless thee - and I shall lead thee into the place wherein I am, and ye shall be glad for thy preparation - so be it and Selah.

I say: Ye shall walk with me, and talk with me, and ye shall be as one lifted up. Ye shall know no want, nor shall ye perish.

I say: It is my part to give unto thee the law, and it is thy part to walk in the way set before thee.

Ye have not heard that which has been said; therefore it is repeated over and over many times, and in many ways, that none might be found wanting.

So be it that I am come that they might all be spared the suffering which shall come upon the Earth.

I am of a mind to deliver thee out - yet I say: Ye shall do thy part, and alert thyself, and be unto thyself true, and force not thy responsibility upon another, for it is the law: EVERY MAN, WOMAN AND CREATURE upon the Earth is self-responsible. And it is said over and over many times: "Be ye as one responsible for thy own salvation".

Ye are thy OWN SAVIOR - none other have ye - such is the law.

I say: "There are no laggards in the House of the LORD".

So be it I have spoken. Amen so let it be.

I AM Sananda

Recorded by Sister Thedra of the Emerald Cross

I Shall Bring Thee into the Place of My Abode

Beloved of My Being:- Blest are thou, and blest shall ye be; I am come that ye may be blest. I say unto thee: Ye shall be forever blest, for it is now come when ye shall walk and talk with me, and ye shall know me as I know thee. So be it and Selah.

I AM the KING of GLORY, and I shall bring thee into the place of my abode, wherein ye shall be as one born of HIM, a SON of GOD, wherein ye shall walk with HIM and talk with HIM, and wherein ye shall know as He knows.

I say ye shall inherit the KINGDOM OF GOD. I say there shall be no secrets from thee; I say ye shall know as HE knows - such is thy inheritance. I say ye have gone out from His place of abode, and unto Him ye shall return. Praise the name of SOLEN AUM SOLEN, it is now come when ye shall be brot out of bondage. So be it and Selah. I am come that ye may be brot out this day.

When ye have set thy house in order, and when thy task is done, I shall bring thee into the place wherein I am, and I shall give unto thee that which has been kept for thee.

I say unto thee, ye shall be as one forever blest. I say unto thee, ye shall be as one which has earned thy freedom. I say, ye shall be as one brot out of bondage - forever free. So be it and Selah.

I say: Ye have gone out as one which has been given free will, and ye have gone into the world of man of thy own free will, that they might be blest of me thru thee. So be it that ye have been unto thyself true - ye have been unto thy trust true, and now ye shall be as one free forever - forever free. So be it and Selah.

I say: Ye shall give this unto them, and they shall bear witness of these my words unto thee - and I use words which they shall comprehend - and I say they shall remember these my words which I say unto thee. They shall bear witness, and they shall remember MY WORDS.

There are none so foolish as the one which thinks himself wise, and none so sad as the one which betrays himself, or his trust. So be it and Selah. I am come that they may have LIGHT, and I work in ways they know not of; I go into the realms they know not; I give unto them in ways they comprehend not. I say they know me not;

yet I AM, and I KNOW MYSELF TO BE. So be it and Selah. I am with thee unto the end.

I AM and I KNOW MYSELF TO BE.

I AM Sananda - Amen and Selah.

Recorded by Sister Thedra of the Emerald Cross

Come Abide with Me In Peace

Beloved of My Being:- Be ye blest of Me this day - draw nigh unto me and I shall speak unto thee, and ye shall give it unto them which are of a mind to hear that which I have said unto thee. I say: Ye shall give unto them the privilege of hearing that which I have said unto thee. Ye shall not deny them the privilege, for it is long past time that they have slept; they sleepeth still, and I say they shall awaken; and they shall be removed from the Earth, for it is now the age when every living creature shall find a new abiding place; and they shall be put into their own environment; and it shall behoove them to prepare themself for a greater part, a better environment - such is progress. I say: Such is progress, and it is that which shall prosper them.

I say: It is NOT worldly goods which prosper them, or make of them SONS OF GOD.

I say: They are the ones responsible for their own preparation, and none shall look unto another for his salvation.

I say: NOT ONE comes save of his own will and of his own effort, and for his effort is he better.

Be ye blest this day, and say unto them as I now say unto thee: "ALERT THYSELF AND COME FORTH AS A SON OF THE ALMIGHTY GOD WHICH HAS GIVEN UNTO THEE BEING". Praise HIS NAME, and give thanks this day is come.

I say: When they lift up their hearts, and when they seek their salvation from the Source which has given unto them their being, they shall be as ones lifted up. They shall be as ones delivered out of bondage forever, for I say that it is the Father's Will that all men be delivered up. So be it and Selah.

Be ye as ones on whose shoulders rests thy own salvation, I am come that ye may have Light. I say ye have walked in darkness lo eons of time, and now ye shall be given aş ye are prepared to receive, and ye shall profit thereby.

I say that none shall force upon thee that which ye are not prepared to receive. Be ye as ones blest to receive me and of me, for I am come that ye might have Light, and that shall be unto thee all which is sufficient unto thy salvation.

It is my part to give unto thee the law, and it is thy part to abide by it, and to walk in the way set before thee. Such is my word unto them - and be ye blest that ye have received me - so shall they likewise be blest.

I am thy Sibor and thy Brother, Sananda

COME ABIDE WITH ME IN PEACE

Recorded by Sister Thedra of the Emerald Cross

31

Father Eternal

"Be Ye No Part of Darkness"

Beloved of my being:- Be ye as my hand and as my mouth unto them, and say unto them in my name that there are none so foolish as the ones which think themself wise. And give unto them this word: While they have slept, the dragon has used them, he has gone the long way to cause them to sleep.

He has given unto them the part which has caused them to sleep; he has tormented them; he has held them in bondage. He has given unto them the portion which he has fortuned out for them, and they have accepted it, and asked of him MORE. I say they have not the mind to ask of ME, the giver of ALL GOOD AND TRUE SUBSTANCE. They have not the strength of their own to stand as the PILLAR of LIGHT which they are - and they know it not; I say they know it not.

Be ye blest this day, and stand as the EVERLASTING SYMBOL OF MAN which I have willed thee to be. Weep not for them which misuse thee - give unto them naught which they can use against thee, and bless them with thy whole being, and give unto them the part which shall be given unto thee for them. And be ye not concerned what they say or do, for it is their own doing, and their own responsibility.

I shall not ask of thee an accounting for them, for there is none which shall be held accountable for the actions and the motives of another. Be ye as one responsible for thy own deeds thy own part, and be ye as one which has been brot out from among them. And be ye no part of their darkness - their foolishness, So be it that they shall arouse themself in due season, and I shall receive them, as the year which brings forth its harvest - all things unto its season.

Be ye as one prepared to be brot in, for it is now come when great and GLORIOUS LIGHT shall flood the Earth, and the power of the LIGHT shall be more than they can bear. And they shall remove themself from the Earth by law, which is the law of LIFE and LIGHT, and no man shall resist it for it knows not change, and for this do they go and come.

Yet I say unto thee: They have no comprehension of the LAW OF LIFE; they put upon it their own interpretations - they give unto the law credit for that which they do of their own WONTON. They offer up their puny sacrifices; they go unto their priests which have ordained themself, which have not the love of GOD within them; they give themself credit for being wise, when they ask of man forgiveness - and they counsel not with ME! I say they know me not!

And they are not of a mind to accept my emissaries which I send out, for they have martyred my prophets, and crucified MY SON. I say they cut themself off from ME. I am within the place wherein I am, as One prepared to receive them when they turn unto me, and bring unto me themself as a living sacrifice, and give unto ME their HEART, HANDS, and their WILL, which I have endowed unto them.

I shall not trespass upon their will, for I have given it freely, and freely shall I accept it - and in turn I shall receive them unto myself.

In the end I shall BE, and I AM without beginning. I AM without end - I AM - I AM thy FATHER ETERNAL;

Spoken: SOLEN, SOLEN AUM SOLEN

Sananda

Beloved of My Being: - Be ye blest this day, and be ye as my hand and my mouth made manifest unto them which are of a mind to receive me and of me, and I shall bless thee. And I shall reveal unto them which do receive my words that which has been hidden from them.

I shall give unto them that for which they have waited, for it is now come when there shall be great changes, and when many shall be removed from the Earth by natural law. And they shall be put into a place provided for them, and they shall be as ones which have created their own environment wherein they shall awaken. I say it behooves them to prepare themself this day, for pity are they which betray themself.

I am one sent of GOD the FATHER that they be prepared. So be it that I shall be true unto my trust, and they shall be as ones which have been given a free will, and I shall not trespass upon it. And they shall be responsible for their own actions and for their choice, for none shall be responsible for them.

So be it that I am the WAYSHOWER, and I can by law but point the way. So be it that there are none which can bear the responsibility of another's sin or UNKNOWING - the result of their "UN-KNOWING", the result of their actions. I say none can accept the responsibility of the salvation of another. So be it that I AM the ONE SENT of GOD the FATHER that there might be LIGHT, and they either accept it or reject it, and be unto themself traitor. Blest are they which accept the LIGHT which I bring. Mighty is the LAW, and swift is the Sword of TRUTH, and the reaper grim.

I speak plainly and with the power of God, for I speak of the law which they know not; and they know me not which go into the dens of the porcupines for Light - I say they know me not! I speak unto thee that they might have Truth, and they look for signs and wonders - they seek phenomena.

They look for miracles, and they see not the hand of God move in the winds, and the waves; they see not the beauty of the snowflake, the rain droplets; they see not the SPIRIT OF GOD move as man made manifest.

They give unto themself credit for being wise, and they cry out from oppression; yet they look afar, and they see not that which is nearer than hand and foot.

They know not that the Father has breathed the WORD which has given unto them being, and they have not been of a mind to turn unto HIM in ADORATION that they might GLORIFY HIM in the Earth - and that they might be lifted up. So be it and Selah. I come that they all might be lifted up. So be it and Selah.

I AM the Son of God, known herein as Sananda

Recorded by Sister Thedra of the Emerald Cross

There Are Ones Which Do Come to Scatter And Divide

Beloved of My Being:- Ye shall be blest this day, and ye shall walk and talk with me. Ye shall now say unto them in my name, that it is finished - it is done! and ye shall add unto that, that there are none so sad as the ones which betray themself.

I say, that wherein I am there are no traitors! I am not so foolish as to sibor traitors. I give not the foolish the pearls of great price. So be it I am as one which knows them, and I see that which they do, and I find their inmost secrets, for there is nothing hidden from me.

So be it that they which do spit upon my words, and set foot against my prophets shall be accountable unto the law, for it is the law. When they give unto themself credit for being wise, I say the law is sure and swift; such is JUSTICE METED OUT by the <u>LAW of JUSTICE</u> which is eternal, and which was in the beginning, and no man shall change it.

Yet every man is accountable for his own part, his own actions, and the law which he sets into motion of his own free will. I am not the maker of the law, yet I abide by it; I create not that which shall torment me; I give not that which I do not want. I care not for their opinions, nor for their coin, for I am sufficient unto myself, and I care for my own - and I bless myself, for I know myself to be one with the SOURCE of all blessings - all GOOD.

I give unto them which serve me as I receive of God the Father, for I am sent that they might be lifted up. Yet I say, when they set themself up, and when they give unto themself credit for being wise, PITY ARE THEY, for they are the greatest of fools. So be it that I

DO WEEP for them! It has been said that I am a man of sorrows - such are my sorrows. So be it and Selah.

I am now come unto thee that they might have these my words, and I command thee: Give them unto them which are of a mind to receive them, and say unto them in my name that there are ones which do walk among them which are of darkness - that which they know not of - which do come to scatter and divide, and which are sent from out the den of the dragon.

And I say too: Likewise are the ones sent of God the Father to deliver them up - to rescue them from the snare of the FOWLER; and he which would snare them is but the one which is of the DRAGON sent; he has many plans - should one fail, he resorts unto yet more ruthless ones. So be it and Selah.

I am of a mind to cast them into utter darkness; yet I say: The LAW is SWIFT as the two-edged SWORD, and the fortune of them which do fall under the yoke of the dragon is sad indeed. So be it and Selah. I command thee: Give this unto them at the earliest possible time. So be it they shall bear witness of these my words. So be it and Selah. I am thy Brother, and thy Sibor, Son of God the Father, Known as Sananda

Recorded by Sister Thedra of the Emerald Cross

To Unit #3

Ye have stood as rocks, and thru the strength you gave forth, the condition in Mt. Shasta was more quickly worked out, than it could have been had you wavered and lost faith.

Many more difficult tests will meet thy Sibors - and weak indeed would we be had we failed in the slight stumbling blocks in our path.

It seems great to thee*, but we are not moved - we will face many greater tests before the new age is established.

Now you will go on - stronger than before, because of thy faith and strength, in passing thru this small rough place on the path to thy attainment. Each one has learned a valuable lessons and this is good for thee and for thy Sibors. What strengthens thee helps all, and all are blest.

Great changes are coming for all; for this ye must be prepared. Ye have asked to serve as needed, and according to thy development. There is to be no square pegs in round holes - all must work smoothly.

No more are we to be used as testing grounds for those unprepared for the work they choose to do. Another will be found to show them their weaknesses, and less time will be lost.

All must discover and know their weakness, for all must have the chance to prove themself.

They had earned their chance, and it was given unto them. So shall they be.

Blest shall ye be for thy faith and strength.

Thy Sibor, Orlando

Recorded by Sorea Sorea,

*The situation in Mt. Shasta.

Note:- Please do not put your own interpretation upon this communication. If it is for you, SPIRIT will reveal it to you. T.

Sananda speaking to Sorea Sorea:

We who walk unseen among thee are not deceived by appearances. We read the heart of each one, and know the true nature of thy being, thy dreams and thy frustrations - thy anxieties and fears.

Can we not lead thee and guide, and be unto thee succor in all times of need? Put thy trust in thy Sibors, and know according to thy trust and faith, no harm shall come nigh thy door. When thou hast learned the truth of all things, ye will laugh at all thy fears, and know the nothingness of worldly wisdom.

Man walks in utter darkness for the most part, and knows not of the great inner plan - the wonderful plan for all life. Nothing is ever lost from the Father's sight.

Prepare ye for the coming great age. Ye shall prepare thyself lest ye spend long ages groping in the dark, as ye have done in the past - SO AGONIZING - SO MOURNFUL!

Is it not time ye grew to thy full estate and abide in Peace and Joy forever? Ye have but to desire and ask, and obey the Father's Will. Walk as He would have ye walk, and ye will see Him face to face. Great will be the rejoicing in the Father's house; be ye not afraid, ye will not be led astray; ye will walk in certainty and with much joy - be ye not afraid.

I leave thee with this assurance: Ye walk not alone, I am with thee always. As I say unto thee I say unto all:

I AM thy older Brother, Sananda

-- Beloved of My Being:- Be ye blest of me and by me, and give unto me credit for being that which I am, and sing PRAISE, and give thanks unto the Father Mother God, that they have sent thee forth at this time to bear witness of these things.

I say that these are the days for which we have waited, and I am glad it is come when we do have this privilege of communication, and this concourse, for I am with thee, and I shall be with thee at the end, for I come that ye may be brot out of bondage. So be it and Selah.

I am thy Sibor and Benefactor, Sori Sori

Recorded by Sister Thedra of the Emerald Cross

Sarah speaking:- Beloved of my being: Be ye blest of me and by me and glad ye shall be, for I come that ye may be blest - and so shall ye be.

Sori Sori shall give unto thee a part separate and apart from this, and ye shall be as one prepared to receive it. So shall it be given unto them which are prepared to receive it; all which are of a mind to receive of him and by him. Such is his part, to give unto them of his love and energy. And when they do receive of him, they shall profit thereby. So be it and Selah.

Sori Sori -- I come as Sori, and I speak as Sori, and as such I go, for I am that. I come with no effort, for I am one with the Father Mother God, and I am not apart, nor do I separate from them.

I move upon the deep; I go within the Earth; I was, and I am the GOD of the wind, of the rain, and of the lightning. I go not neither do I come, I AM, and I am not moved by thy opinions, nor thy wonton. I pre-see that which is to be, for I see all that is and has been - all that shall be.

I am the one which was sent forth as the custodian of the elements which have been - and which was given into my custody from the beginning. I am the keeper of the key, and they obey, and the elements are but my handmaid.

I sing and the wind dances; I write and the ethers record my writing upon the everlasting tablets of timeless substance. I sing and the winds pick up my anthems, and they which have ears to hear, hear that which I send forth for them.

I say: I am the keeper of the KEYS unto the secrets of the elements; I give unto thee the key. I speak unto thee as Sori Sori; born of GOD am I - the keeper of the keys. I speak unto thee as such, and ye shall be entrusted with my GIFT, for I am of a mind to bestow my gift upon thee, for I say unto thee: Ye have used thy gifts wisely and justly; and ye have been as one found worthy.

Such is my part, to give unto thee this part, and ye shall receive this part as my gift, endowed unto me of GOD the FATHER, which has favored me above all other with this office.

I say I am the one favored to be the keeper of the keys; so on thee I bestow MY GIFT as my privilege, and as my right, by divine inheritance. I give unto thee MY MANTLE, MY SHIELD, and MY GIFT unto thee. So be it in the name of the MOST HIGH LIVING GOD. Amen and Selah.

I am thy Benefactor and thy Brother,

Recorded by Sister Thedra of the Emerald Cross

Sori Sori -- Son of God am I, and I speak as man, and in language which ye comprehend. I give unto thee the keys unto the KINGDOM OF EARTH, and the elements thereof. So shall ye accept them in the name of the FATHER MOTHER GOD, and by THEIR GRACE ye shall accept that which is willed unto thee of them from the beginning. So be it and Selah.

Come with me and be ye free from all bondage - forever free. And I say unto thee: No more shall ye be bound by the Earth, and the elements thereof. So be it and Selah.

I come that this may be accomplished, and so shall it be. Amen, and Selah.

I say ye shall place this upon the Altar for a time, and then it shall be sent unto them which have the mind to comprehend; and they shall bear witness of my words unto thee, for ye shall work with the elements, and they shall be thy hand maidens, and they shall serve thee faithfully and lovingly. Such is my word for thy day; and I have spoken, and thou hast heard me. So be it according to the Father's Will - I abide by it. So be it and Selah.

I AM Sori, Son of God, So be it.

Recorded by Sister Thedra of the Emerald Cross

Blessings upon thee my child; walk with me thru the sunlit paths, wherein there is peace and serenity. I come unto thee that ye may know peace such as thou has not known. Blest am I that I am permitted by law to come unto thee; for this have I waited.

I say unto thee: I walk hand in hand with my beloved Brother whom we know, as Sananda, the Lord Jesus Christ of our world/yours and mine.

I say unto thee My Beloved of whom I speak fondly: I call thee MY CHILD, for I have watched thee; I have cherished the memory of our time together, when we walked hand in hand, thru the Elysian Fields, wherein we shared the great joy of our being ONE within the great temple of the SUN;

Wherein we knew the law governing the things which now you are struggling so hard to remember; and because of thy remembering, your longing has been greater;

Yet thy memory remains clouded by the veil of Naya.

Beloved, I say unto thee: Thy memory shall be restored - ye shall remember, and I am GLAD! So be it a great day, and glad shall ye be.

I say unto thee: You and I shall again walk the sun-lit path of the long forgotten temple grounds wherein we last met, and ye shall be glad it is finished. So be it and Selah.

43

I am thy long-forgotten Brother, Sorica

Recorded by Sister Thedra of the Emerald Cross

Sori Sori -- Blest art thou this day, and blest shall ye be. Ye shall now say unto them in my name, that I am one upon whose shoulders rests the responsibility of the winds, and the waters, and the elements of fire. I give unto them that which should give unto them comfort, yet they know me not, nor do they ask of me - the giver of the goodly part. They seek within their own limited world, that which should enable them to conquer the elements; and

it shall be said herein, that the elements are NOT CONQUERED, for they are the fortune of God the Father, and obey the law, even as HIS SONS do obey the law.

I say: The elements shall obey the law of LOVE, and be unto thee thy willing and obedient handmaid, for the law shall govern all things, and ye shall be as ones obedient unto it, OR ye shall be as ones which set into motion which is the reverse of LOVE, and that shall be into thee thy own downfall. I say: Ye shall be obedient unto the law, or it shall consume thee - such is the power of the LAW! Blest are they which serve thee in LOVE, and in peace shall he reign.

So be it and Selah. I am with thee that ye may learn of me, and for this have I spoken of this law of LOVE - and the reverse - which is man's wonton*, his own work, his own bearing. He has turned his face from GOD the Father, and he tries to mock Him. I say God is not mocked, for it is the foolishness of fools. So be it and Selah.

Mighty and unerring is the LAW! And for this we which do keep it are glad, for we weary not in our appointed tasks; we sleep not,

44

neither do we go out from our place of abode. We keep constant watch; yet there are ones which do go out, and which have done so that ye may be confused and tormented. So be it that they are not sent of the Father that ye might be comforted; they are as ones sent of the Dragon, that ye might be held in bondage.

I say: The Dragon is NOT OF A MIND to unleash thee. So be it that we which are sent, come that ye may be freed from all bounds; therefore we speak thusly, that ye shall have such knowledge as which will free thee, in LOVE and OBEDIENCE with the LAW.

The word is but the reminder, and all whosoever receives the word/the reminder unto himself, shall find the truth thereof, for he shall be sibored from the realms of light. Such is the law of the ONE ALMIGHTY GOD, FATHER MOTHER, which has brot us forth in this time; and for all eternity shall we ever be one in them - in the ONE which shall endure - which is without beginning and without end. So be it and Selah.

I am with thee that ye might know thy ONENESS, and be ye conscious of it by day and by night; walk ye in the LIGHT.

I AM SORI SORI

Recorded by Sister Thedra of the Emerald Cross

Rebelliousness

Beloved Of My Being:- I come unto thee this day for the purpose of giving unto thee this word, and ye shall give it unto them, and they shall be as ones prepared to receive it, for it is now come when many shall turn unto the Light, and for this are we prepared.

Say unto them as I would say, that we thy Brothers of Light stand ready to give unto them as they are prepared to receive. And when they have accepted us, and the plan which is now prepared and given unto us for thee, we shall be as ones glad to step forth and reveal unto thee - unto them which have been prepared for such revelation; this plan which has been revealed unto us from the Father's own hands. I say: We are now prepared to step forth as thy older Brothers, which have gone before thee to prepare the way - such is our part.

And it is thy part to prepare thyself to receive us, and ye shall be glad, for we have gone the long way to bless thee; and we are of the Father sent, and ye shall come to know that which is hidden from thee. So be it and Selah.

By thy own effort shall ye be prepared, and ye shall be diligent in thy preparation, and ye shall not turn aside, nor shall ye falter. Ye shall abide in Me, and I shall bring thee out of bondage; and I am sent that ye might be free - forever free, yet ye shall accept me for that which I am, and I shall come in and abide with thee, and I shall counsel thee, and ye shall learn of the WILL of the FATHER MOTHER GOD. So be it and Selah.

I am with thee, and I shall reveal myself when ye are so prepared. So be it and Selah.

Sananda, Son of God, known as Jesus Christ, son of Mary, the ward of Joseph. So be it and Selah.

Recorded by Sister Thedra of the Emerald Cross

Bor speaking:- Be ye blest this day, and I shall speak unto thee of the ETHICS OF SPEECH. I say that there are few which know that

46

which is ethical, and what is prompted by love. I say: Few indeed speak ethically, and few serve the forces of light; for one has but to observe the humanity which does exist within the Earth, and upon it.

And I say: They speak that which is prompted by the forces of darkness, and they bring about their own confusion, and they are as ones which have bound themself in darkness. So be it that they shall come to know the power of the spoken word; and for that am I glad. I come that they may be given such comprehension. So be it and Selah.

I say: This is my part, that they come to know what is meant by ethics, and it is no small task, for they have fortuned unto themself their own opinions, and their own ideas, and seek the they light, shall be given great revelation. So be it and Selah.

Ye shall go unto them and say that which shall be given unto thee to say, and they shall hear the words which shall come out of thy mouth; and they shall be as ones wise to heed them, for the Father shall put words into thy mouth, and they shall be HIS words, and they shall not deny HIM, for HE shall be as thy POWER, thy LIFE, thy SALVATION, and ye shall glorify HIM on the Earth, and ye shall be unto thyself true, and ye shall speak with authority and with power, for HE shall be unto thee all that which is necessary. So be it and Selah.

I am now prepared to give unto thee another part of the Book of DISCIPLINE, and I say ye shall return at a later hour for to record it, and it shall be a new part. So be it and Selah.

Ye shall give this unto them, and it shall be added unto the Temple Scripts; so let it go on record as my part. I am come that they may know me, and my part shall be revealed unto them.

I am not a popular one, for I am the father of DISCIPLINE, and I am now prepared to give them the part which is the extreme and ultimate tests; for wherein is it said: "THERE SHALL BE TRYING TIMES AHEAD"? I endeavor to prepare them to meet these things, and to MASTER such" situations, as they shall encounter.

I say there are none so foolish as the one which thinks himself wise, and none so sad as the one which betrays himself - so be it he is the saddest of the lot.

I see them and know them for that which they are, and I stand ready to sibor them, that they be free forever – such is my part, and it is their part to accept the responsibility of their own preparation, and to prepare themself in the time allotted unto them. So be it the better part of wisdom.

I am thy Sibor and thy Brother, Bor

Recorded by Sister Thedra of the Emerald Cross

Sananda, speaking unto those who have a mind to hear: -

The short time ye have yet to use, must be used for the work of the Hierarchy; not a moment must ye waste - ye must ever be about thy Father's business.

This is not the time for idleness or wasted energy; misused energy is forever lost to the work at hand - be ye ever mindful of this. Thy Sibors work continuously for the fulfillment of the plan - can ye not do thy part?

This is not for the few who are doing all their human natures permit, but for those who sleep or play along the way - so willing for others to do the work.

YE LAGGARDS: Ye shall find thyself crying at the gate, and it closed and locked, for another long age.

AWAKEN AND REPENT! Ye shall be about thy Father's business. This warning I give in LOVE, knowing as ye do not, the terrible consequences of thy disobedience.

I say this - I say that, ever trying to say that which will awaken thee to thy impending peril - if ye do not awaken and stir thyself to aid thy Sibors.

BE YE ALERT! Let not the bridegroom come and find thy lamp unlit, for he cometh when ye know not.

BE FOREVER WATCHFUL! I am the good shepherd; I watch over My Sheep. But when the time cometh, all must be ready, lest the wolf catch one unaware. Ye must keep thy attention upon the shepherd, and be aware of HIM, that He may warn thee in time.

I am ever mindful of thee; ye must do thy part - it is the law - it can not be done for thee.

I come to claim my own; ye must choose; I do not choose who will follow me - and so I await thy call.

BE QUICK!

I am thy Sibor and Elder Brother, Sananda

Recorded by Sorea Sorea (Unit #3)

Gabriel

Blest art thou O my child: Be ye filled with joy this day, and give unto them this my word unto them, and they shall be reminded of me by day and by night, for I am come that they might know me, and that they might be prepared for to receive me.

For thou art my hand made manifest unto them, that they might begin to stir within their slumbers. And I say they shall awaken, and they shall bring forth fruit which shall be acceptable unto the Father Mother God, and unto Him all the praise and the glory. I am that which has come forth that they may awaken from their sleep - and they have slept overtime.

Now there shall be a great voice ring out, which shall awaken them; then they shall hear it; and the ones which do not awaken shall be removed from the Earth forever, and they shall be put in the place which is prepared for them, and they shall be as the traitors unto themself, for they shall begin anew.

And the ones which do awaken, and accept their divine inheritance, shall be as the Sons of God the Father, and they shall inherit the Earth, and they shall be the keepers of the records thereof. For I say the Earth shall move out into her new place of abode, wherein she shall be free from the torment which she goes thru at this time.

50

I say she is tormented, for she is enmeshed within the folds of the great and powerful goat which has come into being in the last century. It is not a goat as you speak of it; it is a great part of the O cycle in which the earth travels, and wherein she shall enter into another, which is likened unto a water jug filled with water - when it is forced from the bottom - topside down, and wherein there is little air.

The Earth has been forced from its place of the *N* wherein she would have her equilibrium and her proper balance; now she reels and rocks as a drunkard; and it is my part to stand guard, that she does not faint and perish.

I say I am alert, and mindful of my part, and I shall not betray my trust, for I am given this part of GOD MY FATHER, and I am glad. So be it that I serve with great joy! and for to glorify HIM, and I am not of a mind to betray myself nor my trust. So be it that I come that they might be reminded of me, and of my part, and that they might be about their preparation - such is wisdom.

I speak as one which has come for this purpose: That they might be spared much suffering. I say: "AWAKEN ALL YE NATIONS OF THE EARTH - PRAISE YE THE FATHER WHICH HAS GIVEN UNTO THEE BEING - BLEST SHALL YE BE".

I AM Gabriel

Recorded by Sister Thedra of the Emerald Cross

Beloved of My Being: - Be ye as my hand made manifest this day, and I do declare for thee thy freedom from all bondage forever. I say unto thee: Ye shall be free forever. So be it and Selah.

51

I say unto them which are as yet in bondage, that it is now come when great changes shall come about, and so swiftly that they shall stand amazed, and confounded, and they shall cry out from fright; while the ones which are prepared shall cry out from sheer joy, for the privilege of being part of this great age - the transition of Earth and MAN. I do declare for the Earth her liberation from bondage, for the Father has willed that all living things shall be free.

So be it that man has caused his own suffering, and he has been his own tormentor - he has accepted his own downfall as final. He has gone out from the Father free, and he has the <u>will</u> to use for his own return. And the law is clearly stated, and recorded. And when he is so minded that he so chooses to obey and abide by the law, he shall be as one free forever; and the Father shall receive him unto Himself, so be it a glad day - I say, glad shall he be. Amen and Selah.

I AM the Son of God, and the One born of Mary - ward of Joseph. So be it and Selah.

Recorded by Sister Thedra of the Emerald Cross

Literal Translation of The Lord's Prayer

as said by THE MASTER

Given by the Lord Mikaal*

"Our Father who dwells in Heaven,

"Glorified be Your Name,

"Your Kingdom come into the World, as it does in Spirit.

"Give to us this day that which we need for our sustenance

"Forgive us that which we do in err, as we forgive those

who err against us."

* * *

We are indebted to:

THE LODGE OF THE SILVER LEAF

OF THE WHITE BROTHERHOOD,

THE GROUP OF SOLAR TEACHING.

*Arch Angel Michael/ Prince Michael

-- Beloved of My Being:- Be ye blest of me and by me - I come that ye may be blest. I give unto thee this part for them which are of a mind to receive it, and it shall not be forced upon anyone; and as they receive so shall they give.

Ye shall be unto them my hand made manifest, and they shall be glad for my part; and likewise they shall remember my servants, for I shall give unto thee that which they shall remember in the days ahead.

I say: I give unto none foolish parts, or foolish sayings; I am as one prepared to give unto them as they are prepared to receive. And they which do accept that which I say unto them, shall be as ones prepared for the greater part.

53

And I do not give my pearls unto babes which do not know their worth. I say: Ye shall be as one which has my hand upon thee, and ye shall be blest of me, and by me; and in turn ye shall be my hand made manifest unto them - yet ye shall not be unto them the scape-goat; ye shall walk with dignity, and ye shall hold high thy head, and ye shall not grovel for a pittance. And they shall be unto themself self-sustaining, and they which do receive of this my work, shall be as ones which have the responsibility of their part of the load. I say that none shall place all the responsibility of this work upon another, yet each unto his part.

Ye shall be as many hand made manifest unto them, and they shall be as my hand made manifest unto thee, for they shall sustain thee, and give unto thee that which is necessary, that my hands be free for this work at the Altar.

And I say unto thee: Woe unto any man or woman which-so-ever that desecrates this my work, or misuses it in any manner whatsoever.

I am now prepared to come unto anyone, wherever they might be, whosoever accepts my words, and to sibor them in my ways - as the Father has willed it, and I pray ye that they might all turn their face unto the Light.

I am with thee unto the end.

Sananda

Recorded by Sister Thedra of the Emerald Cross

Dear Readers :

Again the Masters have reminded us of the seriousness of the times. They have reminded us many times, saying: There is little time left to accomplish what is given unto us to do, and it must not be wasted on the ungrateful ones, the "sleepers".

While I was preparing the next issue for the mail, the Master Sananda spoke saying:

"Beloved: Ye shall say unto them: The time is short,

and there are few laborers in the vineyard, and it

is necessary each do his part; that the load is

indeed heavy, and the servants are few.

When they are prepared for the next part, they shall make it known unto this office, and the next part, or portion will be sent unto them.

And for this shall they receive as it is given, and not one word shall be changed. Such is my word unto them thru thee. Such shall they have, and it shall profit them, for these parts have been blest, and they which take them unto themself shall be blest. So be it and Selah".

Sananda

We the servants, add our Love and labour, that you may be blest by God the Father Mother, thru us.

It is our joy to serve.

Fraternally, Thedra

Berea

Berea speaking:- Blest of my being:- I come unto thee that they may have these MY WORDS, and I say unto them: There is little while left in which they may come unto the Altar, for it is near unto the time when the gate shall be closed, and they shall stand as ones forsaken.

For it is now come when the ones which hold out a hand, shall move on into other fields, and ye shall be as ones wise indeed to meet the day with these words:

"Father, I wait NO MORE, I come unto Thee, and NO false gods shall I have before thee. I shall be unto myself true, and I shall go into the secret place wherein Thou abidest, and I shall counsel with THEE.

I know Thou shall not turn me away.
I ask of Thee, O Almighty Father Mother God:
Give unto me strength and wisdom to discern the TRUE from the false.

I ask of Thee: Be my hand and my foot, for Thou hast given unto me being, and no other God shall I adore.

Behold ME THY CHILD - I come - I give unto Thee all PRAISE, and the GLORY forever, and forever.

I AM, for I KNOW that I AM, and I PRAISE THEE
O FATHER - I PRAISE THEE FOREVER!"

Call with thine heart, and He shall hear thee, and give unto thee as ye are prepared to receive.

I am thy Elder Brother and thy Guardian, who has so loved thee that I wait - I wait with longing for thy return.

Bless thee my own Beloved Sister - my hand made manifest unto them. Berea

Recorded by Sister Thedra of the Emerald Cross

Beloved of my being:- Blest art thou and blest shall ye be, I come that ye may be blest. When I am come unto thee, it is because of thy preparation; and ye have so prepared thyself that ye might receive me, and I am glad.

Now ye shall say unto them as I would say, that there are many among them which are prepared to give unto them the Waters of Life, and they shall prepare themself for to receive it - the substance of Life, from which all things perfect are made. Now when ye are prepared, ye shall drink of the Water of Life, and ye shall step forth from thy body of dense flesh, into thy HOLY CHRIST body as one perfect; and I say unto thee: Ye shall not taste of death. So be it and Selah.

I come that ye might have thy inheritance given unto thee of God the Father Mother - Cause of thy being. Blest are they which receive it in full. I come as one which has received mine, and no man shall make me a pauper; nor shall be take from me mine inheritance. So be it and Selah.

I am glad this day is come, when I can speak unto thee as one being unto another. I am glad for my part, that ye might be brot out of bondage - and so be it.

Know ye this: As ye are prepared so shall ye receive. I am thy Sibor, known as "The WAYSHOWER", and I have gone before thee to prepare the way, so walk ye in it, and ye shall be glad forevermore.

I shall lead thee into fertile pastures, wherein ye shall hunger and thirst no more.

I am the Son of God &&& which ye know not, yet ye have given me names; I am called Jesus of Nazareth, and I am now called Sananda Son of God, wherein I AM.

Recorded by Sister Thedra of the Emerald Cross

Easter Sunday

Beloved of my being:- Blest art thou and blest shall ye be - I come that ye may be blest. I speak unto thee that "they may have these words", and for them are they given into thee. Ye shall be as one blest for this thy service unto the Light of the Christ.

I say: Not one servant goes without reward, for they are that which goes in and out of the dark places, to carry the Light of the Christ. It is the servants which are so necessary unto us thy Sibors; and without thee our servants, we are helpless. Therefore I say: Blest are the servants, and they shall be blest, for they shall be as ones rewarded of the Father Mother God.

Now it is come when they shall awaken, and they shall be as ones which have slept overtime, for much has gone on - been accomplished while they have slept, and they are as ones bound in darkness, and they know not that which has been accomplished.

I say they are blind unto the Light, and they see not, for the Light blinds them while they sleepeth; yet when they awaken they shall see, and they will know that which they see - so be it a glad awakening. I am glad it is now come when they shall awaken, for this have I waited.

I say: I have waited long for them which the Father has given unto me; for this do I give thanks unto HIM, ALMIGHTY, ALL WISE and GRACIOUS FATHER MOTHER GOD. I give thanks this day - bless them which Thou hast given into my care; I AM Thy SON which Thou hast sent forth for to bring them home. So be it that I shall be unto my trust true, and I shall not forsake them, nor shall I betray them nor myself.

So be it and Selah. Blest am I, O MY FATHER MOTHER that Thou hast given me Being; of THYSELF have I come into being, and I am glad. O ALMIGHTY GOD: I do give unto Thee ALL THE POWER and the GLORY forever!

Let Thy LIGHT be made manifest upon the Earth in every living spirit, that all darkness may be dispelled from the Earth, forever and forever - Amen and Selah.

I am come that all darkness might be dispelled - so be it. HALLELUJAH - GLORY UNTO HIM, AND PRAISE HIS HOLY NAME.

Berea (Venus) Speaks

Berea speaking unto thee My Child, that ye may be as my hands made manifest unto them. I say unto them, that wherein I am there is no sorrow, other than thy wonton - thy suffering - thou art our sorrow! Yet ye walk about as ROBOTS, animated by that which ye know not. I say ye shall be as ones quickened, and ye shall come alive; ye shall be as ones willing to hear the voice of thy Eternal Parent.

Ye shall be as ones tormented of thy own longing, and of thy own way, until ye turn unto HIM the SOURCE of thy being, and seek of HIM the LIGHT which is HIS to give. Ye shall be as ones cut off until ye turn unto HIM and ask for thy freedom. So be it and Selah. I say unto thee: Blest are they which turn unto HIM. I say we here in this Temple know the joy of serving Him by day and by night, for we do not sleep; we are alert and refreshed from His own hand; we are not cut off as thou art; we have not cut ourself off as thou hast.

I speak unto thee as one which knows thee and thy way; thy longings have been great, thy suffering pitiful; yet ye have not turned homeward as SONS OF GOD; ye are loath to obey the laws set before thee; ye are loath to be a disciple of the SON -sent of HIM, that ye too may follow Him - the SON OF GOD, sent so long ago. And again and again has he come - yet ye have not been unto thyself true, ye have gone the long way round. Ye have chosen thy way, and none other shall bear the responsibility of thy salvation.

Yet ye shall be as one responsive unto us thy Sibors, which stand ready, and O so WILLING to help thee. Our Love is INFINITE, our strength is of Him the Father; our authority is given of HIM - yet our patience is weakened, and our time is short, for there is much to do, and so little time; I say so little time, for everything is done according unto the law.

Now I say unto thee: The time draws near when ye shall be removed from the Earth, and ye shall be as ones responsible for thy own place of abode - for thy own welfare.

Beloved ones: I stand upon the threshhold of this Temple of LOVE wherein I abide. I speak unto thee from the depth of my being, and I speak as one which knows. I say that in the time which is near, that ye shall be removed from thy place of abode, into yet another, and ye shall be as one responsible for thy own place wherein ye shall be put.

Ye shall hear me, and be ye prepared for thy own place wherein ye shall go. I say, not all places are as thine wherein ye are; not all as mine wherein I am; I say there are many dwelling places within the solar system - galaxies without end.

I say we are free, and not bound unto any one of them, yet we should not be content to be bound within any one of them - for we know what "FREEDOM" means! while ye do not. We see thee as a sad lot; as the little ones in darkness - stumbling in darkness, when there is light abundantly; ye need not wait, the day is at hand.

I say the day is now come when ye shall walk and talk with the SONS OF GOD - the SONS of the ETERNAL LIGHT. They know the Father to be the Source of their BEING; they know the Mother to be the LOVE which sustains them; they know the SONS to be THEMSELF; they are not divided against the ETERNAL PARENT, neither against themself.

They each have a part within the divine plan, and none trespass upon the part of the other, and they are as ones without any quarrel or criticism one for the other. I say they are <u>ONE</u>, and they KNOW that which is the <u>truth</u> which shall set thee free. I say, that within this shall ye be free from all animosity, all hatred, all war, all transgression.

I say: When ye come to LOVE THY GOD, THY FATHER MOTHER, ye shall LOVE ALL THINGS which He has endowed unto thee as CREATION of HIS HAND, as the CREATION of HIS BREATH, breathed out of HIS mouth - made manifest in the world of the seen.

Ye shall be as ones prepared for the "GREATER PART", for ONE shall walk among thee as HIS HANDS and as HIS FEET; and inasmuch as ye prepare thyself, HE shall come unto thee, and He shall touch thee and ye shall be quickened, and ye shall know HIM; and He shall give unto thee a portion which shall serve thee well.

Ye shall be as one free from the gravitation of the Earth, and free from the attraction of the Moon; ye shall have the law of the elements revealed unto thee; ye shall be forever free from all bondage. Ye shall be free to go and come at will into any galaxy; ye shall be ONE with the law of being; ye shall wear upon thy head the crown of the SUN; ye shall walk as a SON; ye shall know thyself to be a SON OF GOD THE FATHER.

And it is again recorded within these Scripts of the SIBORS PORTIONS - and ye have but to ask for them - yet ye shall take the necessary steps to support, to promulgate the work. I say this is the teaching of the Saints, the "SAVIORS" of them which have been directed in the INNER WAY.

I say these are the teachings of the MASTERS, which ye have so vainly sought. I say ye have sought in vain, and for thy own end. Ye have no need to seek further, for ye shall prepare thyself, and the ONE ye would call "MASTER" shall come unto thee, and all thy waiting shall end. So be it and Selah. I speak unto thee thusly, for there is a great need for understanding within thy realm.

I say: PONDER THESE MY WORDS, give unto me credit for knowing that which I say, and I shall be mindful of thee in the days of struggle and trials. I shall speak unto thee and ye shall listen for my voice. Cut out the inharmony of man - close it out. Let LOVE reign supreme - let JOY be within thee, bless them which misuse thee; be unto them a lamp unto their feet.

I say ye shall be unto them a lamp, and I shall give unto thee as the Father would have me. I am thy older sister and thy Sibor, known as Venus. I am the complement of our Beloved Sanat Kumara - Beloved of God. Bless Him for his part, for he is one of thy beloved Benefactors.

Recorded by Sister Thedra

The Water of Life

Beloved of my being: Be ye is my hand made manifest unto them, and say unto them as I would say, that there are many among them which would deliver them out of bondage - should they prepare themself for to receive them.

Now it is come when much shall be accomplished within a short while; and within that time one shall come into the place wherein ye are, and he shall walk with thee, and he shall talk with thee as man. And he shall be as my hand made manifest unto thee, and be as one in authority, and he shall have the power for that which shall be given unto him to do - he shall be as one prepared for his part.

Now in the time left for this part, he shall find many which shall drink of the Water of Life, and he shall be as one qualified to give unto them, as they are so prepared. Blest shall they be - be ye one among them.

I speak of the Water of Life again, for as yet ye know not of this substance. I say it is the Substance of LIFE, from which cometh all things perfect - from which all things perfect are created.

I say ye know not this substance, for ye have not had the purity of heart to use it; ye have not had the mind to use it, for it is "THE PEARL WITHOUT PRICE". I say it is the life substance, which renews and sustains all particles of life; yet ye only condition it - ye do not create anything which is perfect.

I say ye are creators in thy own right - ye create like unto the whore; I say ye create with thy <u>mind</u> like unto thy own - not with the mind of the one GOD FATHER MOTHER, like unto them perfect. I say they are ONE - "perfection" in all that which they create from the liquid substance. I say it is the WORD OF GOD made manifest, and all which do drink of this substance shall become perfect in HIM, of HIM and by HIM, and for His sake.

I speak unto thee again for thy sake, that ye may bear in mind that ye are not without hope - without aid. I say we come that ye may know, and know that ye KNOW, and blest shall ye be.

Be ye blest of me - I am the Wayshower.

I go before thee -

Sananda

Recorded by Sister Thedra m 740A

Beloved of God am I - beloved of God art thou:- I come unto thee from out the heart of God, I am one with the Eternal Parent. I speak with authority; I bless thee as one sent for that purpose; I give unto thee as the Father would have me; I give unto thee that which is my divine right; I give unto thee as ye are prepared to receive.

Now it is come when ye shall bear witness of me, for I shall stand within thy midst, and I shall declare for the thy freedom.

I shall bless thee with my presence, and I shall give unto thee that which I have kept for thee. So be it ye shall be prepared to receive it.

I say: Ye are as ones prepared for this occasion*, for have I not brot thee together? and for the good of all mankind let it be.

65

I say: Ye shall now go forth as ones prepared for the next step, and ye shall be as my hand and my feet made manifest upon the Earth; ye shall walk with me and talk with me, and I shall counsel thee in all thy ways.

Be ye as ones blest, for this day is come when ye may be unto me my hand made manifest, and ye shall be mindful of me, and ye shall be illumined. So be it and Selah.

I say: Ye shall be illumined; so be it the WILL of God the Father. I am now prepared to speak unto thee of many things which will be new unto thee, and ye shall be as ones prepared for to receive it. So be it and Selah.

I say: Ye are as ones blest this day. So be it and Selah.

I AM Sananda

Recorded by Sister Thedra

*Anniversary of the Order of Sarah

Beloved ones whom I have brot unto this altar:- Be ye blest this day, and I say unto thee it is now come when mighty shall be thy power and thy light. Ye shall be as my light - as my voice - as my hands, my feet, for I shall direct thee in thy ways.

I shall speak and ye shall hear, and ye shall respond unto me; I shall bless thee by day and by night; I shall call unto thee, and ye shall hear me, and ye shall rejoice that it is come, when we shall walk and talk together - I shall direct thee in all thy ways.

I shall give unto thee a part separate from all others; I shall give unto thee the part which I have saved for thee; I shall give unto thee as I have received; I shall do all these things and more; I shall bring thee into the place wherein I am, and instruct thee in the ways which I know.

I shall be unto thee Sibor, and I shall give unto thee that for which ye have waited. So be ye as one prepared for to receive it. Thy waiting shall end - so let it be now, and I shall be glad.

Go thy way in peace; I shall speak with thee again this day, and be ye as one prepared to receive me.

I AM Sananda

Recorded by Sister Thedra

The part of thy Sibors is to instruct, it is yours to learn - ye are here for that purpose. Open thy minds and hearts to all that is given thee; be diligent in thy practice of this work which is given thee. We do no idle thing, nor speak idle words - we are serious, and this is serious work.

Ye shall be helped in all ye do, if ye but respond to that which is given thee. We who work on this side of life are not able to do your work - ye must do all that is asked of thee, that this work shall be done in accordance with the plan.

This is serious times, and it is the greater part of wisdom that ye be alert and obedient. We ask of thee obedience above all; ye must be obedient and do the work; ye are not to neglect the calls that are given; ye will be blest according to thy effort, and answer, to the voice of thy Sibors.

We are awaiting thy cooperation; <u>be ye alert</u>, and ye shall have thy reward.

I AM thy Brother, Bor

Recorded by Sorea Sorea.

(The two messages above were recorded simultaneously)

Beloved Child:- I bring unto thee mineself - I breathe forth my will, I speak the Word and it is made manifest. I say unto thee: Be ye made perfect, even as I sent thee forth. Blest art thou this day, go ye forth with surety that I AM. I AM thy Father which has given unto thee being; I breathed thee forth from out my being; I sent thee forth as my breath. I say unto thee: Be ye as my voice - as my hand made manifest unto them which have not the memory of me, of their day with me.

I say unto them: They shall be as ones which have a free will, which is their inheritance, and I say they shall return unto me of their own free will; and I say, I shall receive them unto myself as my own creation - as ones returned unto me. I shall be satisfied when they all return unto me - I shall be filled.

From this day forward, ye shall be mindful of me, and that which I say unto thee, and thy mind shall be MY MIND, and thy voice shall be my voice - and thy hands shall be MY hands; and ye shall have the place which ye shall have, given to do my work which I will that ye do.

I say ye have gone forth as one perfect, and unto me ye shall return - unto me perfect. I speak the WORD, and ye shall be made perfect even as ye went out. Blest are they which return unto me.

I AM thy Father Solen Aum Solen

Recorded by Sister Thedra

As I speak unto thee this night, I give unto thee words for all who have a wind to listen. The time draweth nigh unto all life, when all will see changes - and will be changed; many will find their places in the higher realms. But O so sad! many will be found sleeping, and will awaken in a far sadder state of being - these are the ones who think themself wise - and do not listen to the words of warning, given by the Brothers of Light.

I walk ever by the side of those who call unto me, and I hear all who ask of me in faith and sincerity.

Thou who sit here this night, have been called here to learn, and to be taught, that ye may help thy Sibors in answering the calls for help. Many will call as the time comes ever nearer, when all shall be taken from that which is known to them, and taken to places strange, and in many cases fearful and disturbing. The calls will be heard, and all who call shall be heard. Be ye prepared to assist, and walk no more in darkness, for light will be given to each, according to the need and worthiness. Go in obedience, and serve thy Sibors as ye are called. I give ye this word in love, and peace to thee.

I AM thy Brother and Sibor, Sananda

Recorded by Sorea Sorea

Sanat Kumara speaking: -

Beloved of My Being:- Be ye blest of me and by me, for it is come when this shall bear fruit, and ye shall be as one blest of me, for I shall give unto thee a part which shall be for the good or all mankind - and ye shall be unto then my hand made manifest. I say: I shall give unto thee a part which shall be for the good of all mankind, and ye shall give it unto them, for it is now come when great shall be their need. So be it that I am come that they may be helped; I give unto them as the Father would have me. So be it and Selah.

Blest shall they be; I say they shall be blest; with this shall ye go unto them, and ye shall need no other authority, for it is the sign and the insignia which they shall come to recognize - I say it is my seal, which I give unto thee. So be it the seal I am given of the Father for thee. I come unto thee that ye may receive of Him, for I am sent - even as Sananda our beloved Benefactor - that ye may receive of the Father. So be it and Selah.

Be ye unto them that which I am unto thee, and ye shall goes one in authority, for have I not given unto thee my word of command? I speak unto thee as the Father has commanded me.

I now command thee in His name: Go forth, commanding of them obedience unto the law; and say unto them in the name of the Father Son, that they shall walk in the way set before them. I say they shall turn neither to the left nor to the right, for I am not of a mind to sibor fools, for they are the laggards, which are of a mind to sleep,- and they will have their day.

This is the day of the Lord, when they shall alert themself and come forth as the Sons of God. They shall be their own saviors; they shall have no false gods; they shall be obedient unto the law set down within these Scripts.

I say, these are not the only scripts, yet these laws cover all that is written - or shall be - and I say, blest shall they be which are prepared, in the day of the coming of the KING, for mighty shall be His Word, and exacting the law. Be ye as one prepared.

I AM thy Brother and thy Sibor

Sanat Kumara

Recorded by Sister Thedra

Brother Bor speaking:-

Blessed art thee, and blest art they who gather at this altar; continued obedience will bring greater blessings. Obedience and order must prevail in this temple; it is upon this foundation that this temple will grow - it depends upon thee.

The temple will not fail; others will take up the task if ye fail; be ye alert and walk ye in the way set down for thee, and thy blessings will be in like measure.

It is not an easy task, but help is ever at thy call. Remember, we thy Sibors, are with thee, and will not see thee fail, if ye do thy part. In this temple all do their part; each has his place and his task. Ye which are from this temple go in peace, knowing our hand is upon thee - guiding and aiding thee.

Thou will not fail if you are alert, and do not let self-will take over, for that is the door thru which the dragon makes his entrance - as ye have seen. Ye shall walk in the LIGHT. I will help thee.

I AM Brother Bor

Recorded by Sorea

Beloved :- I come unto them at this time for the purpose of saying that which is given unto me of the Father Mother God. I bless thee this day with these words: "SOLEN AUM SOLEN"; I say BLEST BE THE NAME OF SOLEN - Glad shall ye be for this day; I come unto thee that ye be blest - for this do I come. Great and mighty is the Word SOLEN AUM SOLEN; Praise His Holy Name; give unto Him praise and thanks. I say unto thee: ALL THE GLORY IS HIS.

Be ye as one prepared for the greater part. I say unto thee: Praise the Father Mother God; unto Him all the PRAISE and the GLORY. I am come that ye may know such joy, and I shall be glad this day is come - Amen and Selah.

I AM Sananda

Sarah speaking:- Beloved: One year past I called thee together, and I say unto thee, ye have heard me. This day do ye do thyself honor; honor have ye done unto me; I say, ye have given unto me cause for rejoicing.

I say I am glad, for ye have been unto thyself true; ye have gone the long way to bless them, and ye shall bless them day and night, and ye shall be as one blest of me and by me; for inasmuch as I bless thee, ye shall in turn bless them.

I say: I give unto thee that ye might be unto them my hands made manifest unto them which know me not. Be ye blest of me and by me, and I shall remember thee by day and by night. I come unto thee as thy Mother Sarah - THY ETERNAL MOTHER GOD, FROM WHICH YE HAVE GONE OUT. Command of them obedience of the law, and they shall be brot out of bondage forever - so be it the Father's Will. Walk ye in the Light, and ye shall be brot out. I AM Sarah, Mother of Abraham

Recorded by Sister Thedra

Beloved Ones: Ye come unto this altar in obedience and humility; the blessings shall go out from this temple to all who are open to receive; the vibrations draw all who are of a mind to receive of the higher messages, for this is the highest, or one of the highest upon this planet; and many are not able as yet to receive of this strong meat for yet another age.

Those who are ready must be reached; none can be lost because of lack of opportunity to find their way - or heed the warning being sounded forth from all the four corners of the Earth; it must be sent forth until all hear, and either accept or deny the call to freedom. Many are not prepared, and they will have all the time they need in the place prepared for them.

But ye are the Wayshowers; ye are the salt of the Earth; upon thee and others like thee, the fate of all these souls depend for their freedom. So be ye about thy Father's business, and let nothing stop thee from doing that which is given unto thee to do. Ye have been faithful, and ye shall have thy reward, my obedient children; my love and my strength goes with thee, and I am ever mindful of thy needs - GO IN PEACE AND LOVE. I AM Mother Sarah

Recorded by Sorea Sorea

Sarah

Behold me - I come unto thee this day as one prepared to give unto thee the greater part. Have I not said that I stand ready to receive thee unto myself? Be ye as one ready to return unto me and be made whole. I am within the place wherein I am prepared to receive thee, and many await thy coming, and there shall be great rejoicing; when ye return it shall be a glad day. Praise ye the name of Solen Aum Solen.

Praise ye - all the people of the Earth - PRAISE YE THE NAME OF SOLEN AUM SOLEN, One which has given unto thee BEING. Bless HIM which has sent thee forth, for this day shall bear fruit.

I come that ye may be prepared to bring them in, even as I shall bring thee in. So shall ye give unto them, even as I give unto thee, for have I not said: Ye shall be unto them MY VOICE - My hands? Ye shall walk among them as myself - as my feet ye shall walk; ye shall administer unto them in my name, and ye shall bless them as they have not been blest.

Ye shall go out among them and they shall be healed, and they shall be sifted up. Such is my word unto thee. Now say unto them in my name, that they shall be obedient unto the law, before they shall reap the benefits thereof. I say: They shall be about the preparation of themself - they shall be true unto themself; they shall walk according to the commandments set down before them; they shall go out as an example of the initiate of the temple. They shall carry their head high; they shall bow down unto no man, and they shall know wherein they are staid. They shall be as ones on whose head rests a crown, and they shall walk which way it tilts not.

Be ye not critical of them which do fall and perish, for they are but weaklings which cannot endure - they shall wait until they have grown in spirit and in strength, yet they shall be as the little ones sleeping; while it is given unto others to be up and about the Father's business.

I say they shall not know that which goes on while they sleep; they shall dream dreams which shall torment them, and they shall sleep a tormented sleep! yet I say they shall awaken and come forth as the pea from the pod. Bless the unknowing ones - be a lamp unto their feet. Amen so be it.

I AM Sarah, Mother of Abraham

Recorded by Sister Thedra

Beloved of My Being:- Be ye blest of my being, and I say unto thee: Ye shall be blest this day, and ye shall bless them in turn. I say ye shall be blest, and likewise ye shall bless them. Go unto them in my name and give unto them this word, and they shall bear witness, that there shall be a place wherein many shall gather for the purpose of learning of me, and therein shall be a great pillar of light - wherein I shall stand - and I say they shall not be able to look upon it, for its brilliance shall blind them. They shall fall upon their face, and they shall bury their face in their hands, and they shall be filled with fear, for they shall have great fear and trembling; they shall run and hide themself, and they shall run as rats, running into their hiding places.

Be ye as ones prepared for the entrance, for I shall come, and I shall speak as man, and they shall hear my voice, and they shall be glad. I say: Not one shall be missed; everyone shall be found and given unto - as he is prepared to receive; I say, as he is prepared so shall he receive.

I speak unto thee of this, that ye may be alert and about thy preparation, for it is now come when I walk upon the Earth as the Son of God the Father, sent forth of Him, and by Him. I come at His behest; I go out at His command, I say I go out at His command, and I come unto thee - for He has willed it.

Blest are they which receive me. I am come that there may be Light. So be it and Selah.

I Am Sananda - known as the Nazarine

Recorded by Sister Thedra

Service

Beloved:- I speak unto thee of SERVICE. I say unto thee: Ye shall be unto them my mouth, my voice, my hand made manifest unto them. Ye shall say unto them, that in the days just ahead, one shall go out from the place wherein I am, and he shall come unto thee, and he shall instruct thee in the new part which shall be given unto thee, and ye shall be unto them My hand, and My voice; and ye shall lift them up, and ye shall heal them, and ye shall do all manner of good works in my name; and ye shall not want, for I shall be unto thee all things.

I shall give unto thee that which I would have thee be. I say I shall make of thee my emissary, and I shall give unto thee the authority and the power to lift them up, and to heal them.

I shall bless thee, and in turn ye shall bless them - so be it thy new part. I am SANANDA, SON OF GOD; I speak for the Father which has invested within me my Sonship - my authority. So be it and Selah.

Sananda

Recorded by Sister Thedra

Brother Bor

The light becomes brighter, and as it shines more brightly the vibrations become higher, and those of low vibrations are greatly disturbed; even nature is disturbed, and you have these extremes in weather, which ye are now experiencing. These conditions will grow ever more noticeable, and more extreme. Be ye not disturbed, for as ye walk in obedience, nothing shall come nigh thee to do thee harm.

Being taken painlessly from the body is not harm; ye may find it a great blessing, as many have; with far grander work to do than ye could do on the Earth in a physical body with limitations. Travel is free on the higher plane in which I fortune myself to dwell, and we can visit many places in a short time; with so much to be done, this is a real advantage. You would be surprised to see the things we do; and we play not, neither do we sleep.

But to accomplish our work, we must have ye there, doing your part; and ye must be alert and obedient to that which is asked of thee, for ye are channels to the children in bodies, who must awaken, for it is fast coming, and the time is near when they must arise and be about the Father's business, lest they sleep past the time, and are left behind for another age. There will be much weeping and gnashing of teeth, but time will not turn back, and nothing can be done to ease their agony. Be ye warned.

I AM thy Brother Bor

Recorded by Sorea Sorea

Sananda speaking:-

Beloved ones:- I give unto thee this night words of living truth - words that will never change. Ye are in the last days of this PISCEAN age, and blest ye be to be part of this great time. Many chose as did you, to come into Earth this time to serve, and to finish thy tasks, that ye might find eternal freedom. Many will accomplish their purpose and return to the Father's house, forever free of the wheel of rebirth. Ye are chosen ones - blest indeed of the Father's hand. Ye have gone the long way, and the time of thy trials and grief is drawing to a close. Rejoice My Beloved Children, for ye have much to rejoice about.

Ye are doing the Father's will; ye are obedient; ye do that which is asked of thee with a gracious heart. Blest shall ye be, and as ye journey to your homes, my hand will be upon thee, and I will protect thee, and all will be well with thee. When ye have returned to thy homes, ye will find yourselves in better spirit and illumination, and I give ye assurance that much has been accomplished that ye know not of.

My Peace and blessings I give unto thee my faithful ones.

I AM thy Brother and thy Sibor, Sananda

Recorded by Sorea Sorea

Beloved of my being:- Behold me, I say behold me; I stand before thee; ye see not as man, yet ye know I am with thee - I come that ye may know - I say that ye may know. I come that ye may be blest. I say unto thee: Be ye as one which has my hand upon thee, and I say unto thee, I am with them which I brot, and which I sent back unto their respective places of abode, and I give unto each a different part; yet they shall work as "one"; they shall be as ONE in spirit, and they shall be as one in heart; they shall walk side by side, knowing themself to be sisters, and they shall not go against the law; they shall not be divided against each other, or against themself - they shall be of ONE MIND.

They shall be mindful of the law set down; they shall be of a mind to learn, and they shall not deny that which is said unto them. They shall listen for my words, and they shall hear. So be it and Selah.

I come unto thee that they may be blest this day, - they go their way in peace. I am the PORTER at the gate, and I shall see that no harm befalls them. Be ye blest, for I shall be unto thee both food and drink; I shall be unto thee raiment and light; I shall be warmth and comfort, yea, I shall be unto thee all things which-so-ever ye ask. I give unto thee my Scepter, my Orb.

I am prepared for this part; so be it that ye have prepared thyself for to receive me; and as ye are prepared so I come, I come, I come - blest be this day.

I AM Sananda, Son of God

Recorded by Sister Thedra

Sarah speaking;-

Beloved Children - Children of my heart:- I say unto thee this day: Be ye as ones blest of me and by me, for I come that ye may be blest. And ye shall now say unto them which have been brot here, that they shall be as ones prepared for the greater part, and they shall give as they are prepared to receive.

Yet I say: They alone are as ones responsible for their preparation; they shall obey the law; they shall be unopinionated; they shall be of a mind to learn; they shall be blest for their efforts.

I say I see them as they are, and not as they appear to be, and I am ready to reveal unto them that which has been hidden from them. I say, I shall reveal that which has been hidden from them. Now ye shall be unto them my hands made manifest unto them, and ye shall say unto them in my name, that they shall walk in the way set for them, and they shall be unto themself true; they shall not misuse the energy which is allotted unto them.

I say: Ye shall give thot unto the law, and heed that which is written. Be ye as one which can hear me, and give unto them that which I say unto thee.

I say: "THEY SHALL LISTEN FOR THE WORDS SPOKEN UNTO THEM". They shall be as ones prepared to hear, yet they shall listen, and I shall speak, and they shall not be deceived, for I shall quicken them, and give unto them comprehension.

I shall place within their hand the Rod, which shall become brass; and ye shall be as my hand made manifest unto them; and they shall be as ones wise indeed to heed that which is said, for it is just the beginning, and the preparation for the greater part.

I AM thy Mother Sarah - Mother of Abraham

Recorded by Sister Thedra

Beloved:- Ye depart from this place - yet ye shall return unto this place in the time which is near, and ye shall do thy work as ye are required in this place; and ye will be my hands and my feet made manifest.

And ye will serve with honor, and dispatch all that is required of thee. Unto thee will be given the gift of healing, and ye will see - and hear.

Ye shall be able to live in this damp climate, as ye live in the desert; thy body shall be renewed, and in no way deter thee from that which ye are given to do.

Go ye in peace, KNOWING that I have my hand upon thee and thy beloved Sisters. No harm will come unto thee, if thou art faithful to thy Father Mother God, and to thy Sibors.

I AM thy Brother and thy Sibor, Sananda

Recorded by Sister Thedra

Mother Sarah speaking;-

Beloved ones:- We see thy hearts, and we know thee; and I say ye are steadfast as the mighty ROCK - and ye are the chosen ones. We have not chosen thee; ye have chosen to do the Father's will, and to serve HIM - and all LIFE - and thus ye have chosen.

Blest thou art, and blest shall ye be, and my hand shall guide thee thru all things, and ye shall be unafraid.

Go thou in the Father's service as ye have come. - protected and guided.

Be ye obedient, prompt, and ever conscious of thy Sibors; ask and ye shall receive all that ye are in need of.

My Beloved Children I BLESS THEE.

I AM Mother Sarah

Recorded by Sister Thedra

Thedra speaking:- Thus closes the first year in the service - and dedication, in the Order of Sarah. We renew our energy, and bring ourself to the altar of service, as a living sacrifice - that the Father's

Will may be done in us, thru us, by us, and for us. Inasmuch as we ask for ourself we ask for all mankind. O Father CAUSE it to bs done - we ask it in Thy Name - Selah.

Blood Stained Hands

Beloved Ones -- This day let it be said - that there are ones which know not that I AM COME -- While I say unto thee: I AM COME -- I AM the ONE sent that there be Light -- And it is time that they give up their ways of slaughter and hatred - and turn unto ME -- I tell thee of a surety that their ways shall profit then naught - while Mine Way is the Way of deliverance - Peace and Love -- It is said: "Love ye one another" - yet what do I find? ---

They go into battle - as ones in "royal robes" as ones pure - and consumed with a holy purpose -- I say unto thee: their hands are stained with the blood of their fellow men --Yea - unto this day they are given unto murdering their "Saints" - the ones which do crusade for a "Holy Cause"! -- They persecute the ones sent as messengers -- They run from them - and fail to support them - and the Holy Cause - while they spend untold amounts on the slaughter of their brothers -- Yea - I say: "Brothers" deny not mine Word -- Know ye that I KNOW that which goes on within the "World of men" -- I tell thee: they are not blameless -- They have their hands stained with the blood of their own Brothers - for BROTHERS are they! -- They are from the same root - the same Source -- I say they are from the same root - and they are brothers -- Let it be said - they shall answer for their guilt!! ---

Let it be recorded - that which I have spoken - and they shall come to know that they are the "Fools and the Traitors" - that they

have sold their birthright for a counterfeit quarter - a <u>poor</u> <u>penny</u>! --
-

Now I say unto them: - Ye shall lay down thine arms - and ye shall take up the Cross and follow ME -- Ye shall be responsible for thine every act -- And ye shall atone for all thine deeds - yea - even unto the last -- Ye shall be as ones free - when thou hast atoned for ALL thine misused energy -- So be it and Selah ---

I AM Sananda

The Lord God - sent of Mine

Father - Solen Aum Solen

Recorded by Sister Thedra of the Emerald Cross

Horrors of The End Time

Behold - Behold! the Glory of the Lord! -- I say unto thee - Behold the Glory of the LORD! - and know ye that the time is now come when ye shall see the Work which I shall do - for I shall show Mine hand! ---

I shall do a <u>Mighty</u> <u>Work</u> - and NO MAN shall stay MINE hand - for it shall pass over them as a Mighty Power - and that power is not to be pilfered or nullified! ---

I say the "Power" of which I speak shall NOT be pilfered - or nullified - for it shall be as nothing seen by man -- I say: they shall BOW DOWN and SEEK THE LIGHT - Which I AM -- For they shall come to know that they <u>are</u> not <u>self</u> <u>sufficient</u> - sufficient unto themself ---

They shall cry for the help of the Power from and of the MIGHTY HOST -- They shall <u>bow</u> <u>low</u> - as ones prostrate before their King -- They shall plead for help - for they shall be betrayed by father - by son - by brother - sister - mother - and by the friends -- I say these are the days spoken of - of old - as the "End Times" - the "End Time" which shall bring great divisions of all people -- And they shall run riot! ---

And they shall be as the beasts of the field -- They shall eat as the beasts -- They shall sleep as the beasts -- For many shall have no place wherein to lay their head - no place wherein to rest their weary feet -- So be it that I have spoken unto thee - that ye might know wherein thou art staid -- So be it that I AM COME that there BE LIGHT -- So let it BE ---

I AM Sananda

Recorded by Sister Thedra of the Emerald Cross

Sanat Kumara Speaks to the Ones in The Temple of Sananda & Sanat Kumara

Beloved of Mine Being -- Hast it not been said that it is given unto Me to be the Lord of Venus? - it is SO -- Yet I Am no less - for having taken unto Mineself the custodianship of the Earth -- For long have I gathered Her unto Mine bosom -- I have watched Her thru Her many <u>perilous</u> <u>times</u> - and I have taken responsibility for Her safety ---

Now it is come when she shall reel and roll - as a ship - storm tossed at sea -- Yet I say unto thee She shall survive! -- For this have I given of Mineself that it be so ---

Now wherein is it said that - "She shall be given a new berth?" -- It is now prepared - within the roadways of the heavens -- The way hast been cleared - that She might have a port wherein She might be renewed - and have surcease from Her groanings -- She shall no longer be tormented by that which hast been fortuned unto Her by and thru the LAGGARDS ---

She shall be freed of them - for they shall be put into yet another place - wherein they shall first learn the responsibility of their own deeds ---

There shall be a resting period for the Earth - for long hast She groaned under Her burden -- Yet She hast done Her part grandly - and <u>Victory</u> shall be Her reward -- So be it I give unto thee this Word that they might have it at this time - for it is the time of great anxiety and change -- Change is good - and it behooves Me to remind thee of the changes - for there is no stagnation within the Realms of Light -- So be ye as ones prepared to go forth to meet such changes with a glad heart -- Let it BE as the Father Wills it -- For art thou not of the "First Born"? ---

SO BE it and Selah --

I AM Sanat Kumara

Recorded by Sister Thedra of the Emerald Cross

All Shall Be of One Mind

Beloved Ones -- Let it be understood this day - that I AM the ONE sent that there be Light within the realm of darkness -- For I say it is thru and by the Light Which I AM that the world of man shall come out of darkness - out of its bondage - out of the pit! ---

Now it is accredited unto ME as being the "Savior" of the world -- While it is so - it is not fully understood that each and every one hast his own responsibility for himself - and his actions ---

Each and EVERY ONE has the responsibility of preparing himself for the NEW DAY - the day of revelation - wherein he might be as one responsible for the NEW revelation - the power and the authority which goes with such revelation as I bring ---

Now it shall be given unto each one which chooses Mine Way - to have the power and the authority which is Mine -- For they shall be as equal unto Me - in Mine Fathers Kingdom -- They shall be Co-Creators with HIM - and He shall give unto them the power and the authority which is like unto Mine - for therein is no inequality -- There is no preference - no favor shown -- Each shall choose freely his work - his part - which shall be according unto the GREAT and DIVINE PLAN - and none shall oppose it - for ALL shall be of ONE MIND -- One part - one mind - that of serving the WHOLE - for the GOOD of ALL ---

Now when it is said that there are many within the "MIGHTY HOST" - it is SO -- And yet they are not divided amongst themself -- They have no thought other than to serve the Whole of the Plan ---

The Plan is the fulfilling of the part which hast been given unto thee from the beginning -- It is the Way which hast been designated for man - which enables him to find his way home - yea - to make his ascent from out the pit ---

I say unto thee - man hast created his own pit - and hast fallen into it headlong! ---

I AM COME that he be delivered out -- Yet he shall will it so -- So be it he shall first be obedient unto the Law which I bring -- He shall make ready himself to receive Me - and then I shall give unto him as he is prepared to receive -- So be it I do not betray MINE SELF or Mine Trust ---

I AM COME that there be Light --

I AM Sananda

Recorded by Sister Thedra

Vacation Time - (May)

Beloved Ones –

This day let it be recorded that which I say unto thee -- It is the time of going and coming - the time of haste and waste -- Yet it is given unto some - to go out seeking wisdom - and others go for yet another purpose ---

Now I say unto thee - the ones which come unto thee seeking wisdom shall be blest -- The ones which come seeking wonders - shall not see the Work of Mine hand - for the Glory thereof shall be hidden from them -- The ones which come seeking shall find - and it shall be their reward -- So let them which come asking of ME - be fed -- Them which come bringing their own offal - shall take it away with them - for they shall in no way contaminate thee -- Give unto them nothing which they can pilfer - or use against thee - for they are the "bigots" and "hypocrites" -- So be ye no part of them -- Let them go their way - and give unto them naught! -- So be it that I have spoken - and thou hast heard Me ---

I AM Sananda

Recorded by Sister Thedra of the Emerald Cross

Zeal and The Zealot

Beloved Ones -- This day let Us speak of "Zeal" - the zeal which consumes them - the zeal which gives unto them no rest ---

This is the misspent energy which is fortuned unto so many ---

This is the mis-directed energy which is so often the fortune of the "zealot" -- Zealots are prone to the work of bringing others into the place wherein they have not yet entered ---

The zealot has as yet not drunken the last drop of his own "portion"* - yet he is want to give it unto his neighbor - that he might sup with him ---

It is said: "First apply the portion unto thine own self - and when thou hast proven its worth - and found the cup sweet - pass it unto thine brother" ---

First prepare thineself - and then thou shall go fetch thine brother - for by thine light shall he follow thee ---

Wherein is it said - <u>let</u> <u>thine</u> <u>own</u> <u>light</u> so shine - that <u>they</u> might see it and be drawn unto it? ---

Yet the blind seeth not -- While the blind shall have their eyes <u>made</u> to see -- So be it that I shall touch them which are so prepared to receive Me - and of Me -- So be it and Selah -- I Am come that they might see - yet there are ones which have not asked of ME ---

They seek of men - their opinions - and they ask not of the Father for Light -- I say: they which ask of the Father shall <u>not</u> be denied - - So be it I AM sent that there be Light -- So let IT BE ---

I AM Sananda

* "The Word" - The Scripts - Sibors Portions - which they pass on to others before they know what they <u>really</u> are - and have gotten the full meaning - tested them - found the hidden "Pearls" within --
-

Recorded by Sister Thedra of the Emerald Cross

The Wanderers Blessing-

Beloved of Mine Being: - I say unto thee <u>this</u> day - that once there was a Prophet <u>great</u> of <u>stature</u> - filled with love and wisdom - which <u>knew</u> <u>his</u> <u>Source</u> - and he wast given unto wandering -- He wandered the LANDS of the EARTH! - as he awaited the coming of the Lord or Hosts ---

He carried with him neither purse or food -- He called no place home -- He had within his hand the power to create for himself the food sufficient unto his need -- He called ALL men Brother -- He carried no penny - no clothing -- He wandered empty-handed - yet he did not want -- While I say he did not want - I tell thee his waiting wast long and hard -- He knew not the hour - the day - the year of the coming of the Blessed Lord of Hosts -- He cried out in his longing - as tho his heart would break! ---

I say unto thee: - Weary not of thine lot - for I say unto thee - the waiting shall bring its reward! ---

Hasten ye not to betray thineself - for I say unto thee - the waiting shall bring a great reward ---

So be it I KNOW - for I AM He - the Wanderer -- I bless thee with Mine Presence -- I go as I come - and I bid thee – Adieu

Recorded by Sister Thedra of the Emerald Cross

Self-Responsibility / Bthe "Threshold of Despair"

--The Wanderer

Beloved of Mine Being -- Let this be a day of great joy - for the time is come when the Mighty Host hast drawn nigh unto the Earth - and it is fortuned unto Me to be One of Them ---

I tell thee - it is a great day - and one in which it is come that all the Host be prepared to go forth as to battle - for within the HOST there are NO LAGGARDS ---

We of the "HOST' or which I speak - are prepared to do battle against the forces of darkness! ---

We are not wanting - for We are well qualified for Our Part -- For this have WE prepared OURSELF ---

Not a plan goes astray -- We know the plan - and are One with it -- It behooves Us to know -- And We are not unaware of the forces which beset the "World of men" -- Yet it is of their own making -- And they shall be responsible for that which they have created -- While it is a sad lot that they are - and their plight is a sad one indeed! - they shall be as ones responsible for it -- They shall learn well their lesson - which is SELF RESPONSIBILITY -- They shall learn that they have the power to create - either for weal or woe - and that is no small gift! ---

Let it be said that there is a way unto their "Salvation" - their deliverance from bondage -- It is clearly written that there "IS LIGHT" - and they have but to seek it - and turn from their OWN puny way - the way which hast lead them into the pit ---

While it is given unto US to see and to KNOW that which goes on within their secret chambers - I tell thee of a truth - We dare not trespass upon their free will - until they cross the "threshold of despair" whereupon they shall be stopped! ---

I say: - There they shall be stopped!! - KNOW YE THIS - "there are none so sad as the one which betrays himself or his trust" - for he is indeed the "Traitor" -- Be ye no part of him -- Give unto him no footing - let him go his way - and hasten ye not after him - for he shall bring about his own end -- Hear ye that which I say unto thee

- and be ye as ones blest - of Me and by Me -- I come as One of the Great Assembly - as One which sees the need - and I have answered it -- So be it I stand with outstretched hand - extended that ALL whosoever will might take it - and I shall give of Mineself that he be lifted up -- So be it -- I AM known as The Wanderer -

Where to Find Safety?

Beloved Ones -- Mine hand I give unto thee this day -- Accept it in the Name of Mine Father which hast sent ME -- I say unto thee: - The time swiftly approaches when there shall be great rivers - run within the deserts -- And the mountains shall give unto "them" no hiding place -- "They" shall flee their abiding places to find no resting place ---

So be it that I Am come to give unto "them" of Mine Love - Mine Wisdom/ Mine Knowledge/ Mine foresight -- Yet "they" turn aside and hear Me not -- "They" are filled with FEAR! -- "They" seek safety within their own realm -- While I say there is no safety within "their" realm - for their realm shall be shaken unto its VERY FOUNDATION! -- And they shall run hither and yon seeking peace - and there shall be no peace ---

For Peace hast not been established within them -- They know not from whence cometh their peace - they KNOW ME NOT ---

Wherein is it said: I AM thine shield and thine buckler? -- SO BE IT - and LET IT BE -- For this have I COME ---

I AM Sananda

Recorded by Sister Thedra of the Emerald Cross

93

O, Father - Blessed Art Thou

O - Holy Father - Father of Mine Being - Giver of Life art Thou -- O - Father - this day I would that they - these THINE Children KNEW Thee as I do ---

Let it BE -- For this have I revealed Mineself ---

Father - Blessed Art Thou - Holy Art Thou - and Mighty is Thine Works -- PERFECT Art Thine Works -- Keep these Thine Children - in the Way Thou would that they go -- Hold them Father - I ask it for their sake ---

Thou knowest them and their <u>every</u> need -- Yet I speak that they might bear witness of Mine Love - Which I bear for them -- For their sake have I bared Mine Cross -- For their sake have I gone out from Thee as "man" -- For their sake have I lowered Mine Light - that they might see that which they are capable of comprehending ---

Give unto them greater capacity for knowledge - O Father -- Let them arise with Me - and return unto their rightful estate - that which Thou hast Willed unto them ---

Thank Thee O Blessed Father - that thou hast heard Me -- I bless them with Mine Presence ---

SO LET IT BE

I AM THINE SON

Sananda

Recorded by Sister Thedra of the Emerald Cross

94

Alert!

Sori Sori -- This is Mine time with thee - and it is the part which I have kept for thee - that I shall now give unto thee -- This is the part which hast been kept for this day -- The time in now - when We shall be as One prepared for that which is to do - - the time is <u>Now</u> <u>Come</u> when We shall do that which is given unto Us to do --

There shall be a place provided for each and every one which goes forth out of the physical body - - each one shall find that he is prepared for the place wherein he is received --

There shall be room aplenty and to spare - - there shall be no rush - no over-crowding -- The way is prepared - each shall be received into his proper place - according to his preparation - so be it the law - and the Plan which is unfolding before thee --

There is not one which shall be out of place - each shall be within his own place - according unto his own preparation -- There shall be a Great and Mighty onrush of Assistants - which stand ready to assist -- There shall be the Ones which have gone before - which have made such progress that they are now prepared to go forth to receive them which are yet to come - the ones which are to come –

This is the Way of the Lord - that each be prepared for his part - his place - - as he is prepared so shall he receive - - as he receives so does he give - he gives in like measure unto his receiving - for as he is prepared - so does he go forth to serve his fellow men --

This is selfless Service - for they which serve the Light Know the value of Service - Know the joy of Serving as they have been served -- So be it that they serve as One - with Oneness of Purpose

- - that each might go forth - that his fellows be lifted up -- So be it and Selah –

Say unto them: There shall be a great gathering in - a great coming in - and it behooves Me to say unto them: "Lift up thine eyes - from whence cometh thine help" -- Ask of the Light that ye be prepared for the Greater Part - so let it profit thee - - So shall it be for the Good of All -- So may it be - as The Father hast Willed it --

I say unto thee: Heed that which I say unto thee - heed ye THAT WHICH I HAVE SAID UNTO THEE - and be ye as One Alert - for the time is NOW COME that ye shall SEE THE HAND OF GOD MOVE -- The tide shall be staid - the air shall be rent - the air shall be as polluted - the flesh shall be torn - the hands shall be bloody - the head shall be as torn away - the parts shall be separated one from the other - and not one shall be left for the vulture -- So be it that I have said: Fire and water shall mix - and it is so -- The mountains shall bow low –

the rivers shall raise up -- yet man shall be as ones prepared for his NEW Place - for it is said: "Man" is Eternal -- man is man - and he comes under the law --

Now it is said: AS YE ARE PREPARED SO SHALL YE RECEIVE --

Be ye as one prepared to follow where I lead thee - that ye might go where I go -- So be it ye shall have no fear - for I Am The Lord thy God Sent that ye be listed up - So be it and Selah --

I Am He Which is Come that ye be lifted up - therefore I say: "Come - seek ye the Light and ye shall NOT taste of 'death' " --

Let this be Mine Word unto them which are of the mind to hear and heed -- So be it that this Mine Word shall go forth that they might Know what I have said -- So be it I have sent it forth - it is valid - and the Word shall stand as a testimony of the Word Immaculate -- the Word shall not become invalid - by man nor time -- For this do I say: "Prepare thyself for the Greater part" -- it is the Law that ye be prepared - that ye be warned -- therefore I say: Heed that which I say unto thee - that ye be prepared - for it is thine own responsibility to prepare thyself -- So be it and Selah --

Recorded by Sister Thedra

Warning

Beloved Ones -- Wherein is it said that the way is now made clear before thee -- It is so -- And no man shall deny thee entrance into the place wherein I abide -- Yet I say unto thee - see and know ye that there is but ONE Lord of Hosts... Lord of Lords - Sibor of Sibors - and none shall be unto Me a puny pretender -- For I say unto thee - the Father hast given unto Me the Place - the Name and the Part which is Mine -- And yet I say there are ones which would rob Me of Mine inheritance ---

And it is given unto Me to know them - I KNOW THEM! -- I say unto thee - it behooves thee to be alert and WISE - for no man taketh away that which is given unto thee -- Yet he but waits for thine door to open unto him -- He would deprive thee thine right or speech - thine action - thine inheritance -- I tell thee it behooves thee to KNOW THEM -- I too tell thee - ye shall know them by their fruit -- Such is Mine Word unto thee this day -- So let it be known that I Am with thee --

97

Recorded by Sister Thedra of the Emerald Cross

And Nothing Shall Be Hidden

Hear ye this day the WORD of the Lord thy God -- And be ye as ones prepared for the things to come -- Know ye that the Way is open before thee -- Yet there are many which would beset thee - which would turn thee from thine appointed course -- Know ye that the time is now at hand - when the door shall be closed upon them which are weak of character - and frail of spirit -- I say unto thee - it is NOW come when the door stands ajar for the STRONG of Spirit -- And the wonton shall not find the latch - for it shall be hidden from the unjust and the imprudent -- Is it not said: "Ye shall seek the Light with thine WHOLE HEART - and nothing shall hide it from thee"? ---

It is now come when ye shall stand firm as "The Rock" - the Rock I have given unto thee - THE ROCK - The Foundation upon which I have builded -- I have given unto thee - now ye shall be as the material of which I shall build "Greater Mansions" -- I shall build EVEN GREATER - and no man shall tear down or destroy Mine handwork - for IT shall endure -- It shall not be vainly used - neither shall the unjust look upon the Work of Mine hand - for it shall be hidden from their sight - While I say unto thee - LOOK - SEE and KNOW ye that I AM COME that the KINGDOM of MINE FATHER be established upon the Earth ---

I AM COME that YE might see and know --

So let IT BE -

I AM Sananda

Recorded by Sister Thedra of the Emerald Cross

Sananda - Credentials & Mission

Behold the Work which I shall do - for it shall be a MIGHTY WORK which shall glorify Mine Father Which hast sent Me -- I say unto thee: Behold! SEE! that which I shall do - for I shall touch thee and thine EYE shall be opened - and ye shall behold the Glory of the Lord ---

Ye shall stand in wonderment - and ye shall praise the Name Of Solen Aum Sol Which has sent Me -- So be it I come with the rod and with the Crown -- I come with POWER - with the Authority which IS MINE -- By Divine right I come unto thee as the "First Born" "The King of Kings" - the "SON OF GOD" "The Wayshower"-- I come unto thee as One prepared to give unto thee as I have received -- I come as One qualified to deliver thee out of bondage ---

So be it that I AM the Lord thy God - And there is but ONE LORD GOD -- So be it many shall mimic Me - and come declaring they are thine deliverer - and they shall be so bold as to use Mine Name -- Mine Words shall they pilfer - that they might deceive the unknowing ones -- So be it that I am NOT to be mocked - for these which come declaring falsely shall be exposed for that which they are --- And I say unto thee: be ye as one blest to KNOW the true from the false - <u>For this have I revealed unto thee Mine Precepts - and I have given unto thee that which shall suffice</u> ---

Let no men deceive thee - for I Am come that ye might KNOW the TRUTH -- So be it and Selah ---

I AM

Sananda

Recorded by Sister Thedra of the Emerald Cross

Let It Be Known

Beloved Ones -- This day - let it be known that I Am come - come into the Earth as man -- While I Am not AS man - I Am that which is the MASTER -- <u>I Am the</u>

"Wayshower" -- I have overcome flesh -- I Am that I choose to be - for I Am One with the ALL - The Eternal Father ---

I know Mineself to be One with Him - for I have not separated Mineself from Him ---

I know Mineself for that which I AM ---

<u>I go not - neither do I come - I AM</u> -- Yet it is said: "I come unto thee" - So be it - for I surely give unto thee of Mineself that ye right be lifted up - that ye might know that which is hidden -- I say - I reveal Mineself unto thee for the purpose of bringing mankind out of their bondage - out of their darkness -- Let it be said that I reveal not Mineself unto the unjust and the imprudent -- Yet they shall see that which I shall do - for I shall do a wonderous Work - and they

100

shall marvel and mumble among themself at the Work which I shall do - for I shall set free Mine People -- I shall cut loose the part which has held them captive -- I shall give unto thee lowly - a Voice that they might have a voice in the governments of the lands ---

And I shall be as the One to put within their mouth the words to say which shall astound the "Wise" - for I say unto thee this day - the ones which sit in high places and THINK themsell WISE shall be confounded by that which shall be done -- For I shall do the mighty Work which shall confound them -- I shall bring about a NEW ORDER among the people ---

I shall set up a government for the people - in which they shall be free of bondage -- And I shall pluck out from among the people the ones to be unto Me Mine hands - Mine feet -- I shall give unto them the power and the authority to act as Mine Ambassadors -- I shall give unto them the words to say - and they shall be true unto their trust -- To thee I would say this day - thine part is no small part - yet thine work hast but begun -- Let it be known that which I have said unto thee - and at no time shall ye be censured for thine part --
-

Let them which have a mind to learn of Me - come- and I shall give unto them as they are prepared to receive -- So be it I AM the Lord thy God --

Sananda

Recorded by Sister Thedra of the Emerald Cross

Appearance is The Deceiver

Mine Children -- Upon Mine High Holy Mountain I view the ways of men -- I see and know them - for I AM the Lord thy God -- I know them for that which they are -- I know them for that which they shall become - for I see the END as the beginning -- I say unto thee - the ones I see are varied and many – They are as ones looking afar - for that which is ever present - that which is within their hand ---

They give unto others power to give and to take that which is theirs -- They are wont to see that which is before them -- They ask of man his blessing - when he hast the Eternal Verities within his hand ---

He hast the power which is his to use when he hast become of age - when he hast learned well his lesson - that he might use such power for the GOOD OF ALL -- Let it be understood that appearance is the Great Deceiver - the whore -- I say unto thee - be ye not deceived by appearance - for it is but the outer - and no man seeth that which is hidden from the eyes of the unjust and the imprudent -- List unto Me - O ye children! Know ye that it is now come when ye shall sit with Me in Council - and ye shall be as Ones prepared - for NONE OTHER shall I counsel - for I counsel not the foolish / the unjust -- Be ye as Ones blest this day -- And I say unto thee - let thine own Light so shine that ALL might see it and follow it / that they might know that thou knowest Me - The Lord thy God --

Sananda

Recorded by Sister Thedra of the Emerald Cross

Hold Ye The Light

Hold ye the Light -- Kaow ye that there IS

LIGHT -- Walk ye therein - and ask of no man

that he be unto thee servant -- For I say unto

thee - man is a poor servant - for I the Lord

thy God knoweth thine needs - thine EVERY NEED

So be it I give unto thee that which

thou art prepared to receive - that which

shall profit thee -- So be it that I bless

thee with Mine Being -- With Mine OWN HAND

have I blest thee -- Now I have said unto

thee - thou shall bless others as I have

blest thee ---

So be it that I AM

Sananda

Recorded by Sister Thedra of the Emerald Cross

They Worship the False & Magicians

Beloved Ones -- Mine time is come and I say unto thee: many come in Mine Name - wherein they proclaim great - wonderous words - powers-- Miracles do they perform that they might astound them which know not the false from the TRUE -- I say - they which know not bow down and worship the false and the magician - while I stand by and wait for them to learn well their lessons -- Then they shall have the comprehension which is required of the "Initiate" -- I say the Initiate seeks nothing save TRUTH / LIGHT - and this is that which shall be revealed into them which seek LIGHT"

Let it be said that Light is justice -- Light is the Power through which they shall be delivered up -- I say: The POWER which is the LIFE / the WAY - is that which shall deliver them up -- They shall find that NO MAN is responsible for them -- NO MAN is their Master which taketh upon himself their load / their responsibilities/ their frailties ---

They shall learn that THEY ALONE are responsible for their weakness - And THEY shall learn well that they have no "Scape-goat" -- They shall become the age of responsibility -- They shall be as ones responsible for all their own misused energy -- For it is said - and rightly so - there is no such law as "Vicarious Atonement"! -- No such law hast been given into MAN! ---

For this do I say unto MAN: "Awaken"! Be ye as one responsible for thine own misused energy - "Turn from thine own and seek ye the Light" ---

This I have said many tinies - yet they look afar for a Savior - and easy way ---

I say unto them: Obey ye the Law - apply it unto thineself - and be ye diligent in Its application - and ye shall be thine own savior in the doing ---

Hold high the lamp which I have given - drink ye from Mine Chalice - and I shall give of Mineself that ye be lifted up -- Ye shall do thine part - and I shall not forsake thee in the time of trial -- I bid thee Awaken / Arise / Come - and be ye as Ones prepared to enter into Mine Place of Abode ---

I AM Sananda

Recorded by Sister Thedra of the Emerald Cross

I Hear Them ...Which Cry Unto Me

Beloved Ones -- This day I say unto thee - there are none which have the power to stay Mine hand - for I the Lord thy God shall do a Mighty Work - and they shall see that which I shall do -- While they know Me NOT - they shall see the Work of Mine hand -- And I shall set straight that which hast been made crooked --

So be it that I - The Lord to God hast the Power - and the Authority - the Wisdom to bring them out of bondage -- While they cry unknowingly that I Am come - they cry out for deliverance -- I hear them and I shall find them which cry unto ME - for I say they are Mine People - Mine Flock which are down trodden and suppressed by the ones which have set themself up - them which sit in high places and call themself wise -- Let them be - for they shall

105

be brought low - they shall fall - and be as ones broken -- While Mine people shall arise as on the wings of the morning - and they shall no more war - they shall no more know suppression - for they shall be delivered out ---

I say I shall find them - and I shall deliver them out -- So be it I Am come that it be SO --

So let it BE -

I AM Sananda

Recorded by Sister Thedra of the Emerald Cross

Personality - Individuality

This Day - let it be recorded that which I say unto thee - and it shall profit all which have a mind to follow in Mine footsteps -- It is for this that I say unto thee:

Be ye as ones prepared for the Greater Part -- I tell thee this day - it is the GREATER PART for which thou hast waited ----

Thou hast as yet not tasted of the GREATER PART - for flesh cannot endure that which is kept for thee -- Flesh is the weaker / lesser part -- While the Spirit has not lessened by coming forth as the flesh - that of coming forth into flesh / matter -- Spirit is no less for being the person -- While it is not the person - the personality -- The personality is superficial - and not the REALITY -- The personality is that which is cultivated - and which is come into being from and through experience -- While Individuality is yet another

106

subject - which I shall speak of at another time for which ye shall wait -- So be it that I shall wait for that part -- Let it be ---

I AM Sananda

Recorded by Sister Thedra of the Emerald Cross

I Am Aware of 'The Traitors'

-- Let this be recorded that they might know that which is said unto thee -- Behold the hand of God move -- See it move - and know ye that I Am the Lord thy God -- So be it that I Am aware of the Sons of God / their places / their parts -- I Am aware of "The Traitors" - and their parts which they play with such audacity - with great and pious pomp -- They are wont to be given instruction from and by the forces of Light -- They betray themself - they are not as the Sons of God -- They are not of Mine Flock - for I Am not of them -- I give not of Mineself that they be strengthened ---

I give not Mine Cup unto them - that they sup with Me -- I withhold Mine Cup from them - for they do make a mockery of Mine Words -- They sell their heritage for a poor penny -- And at no time shall I betray Mine trust or Mineself - for I Am come that there be Light -- So let it BE -- <u>Let them which have the MIND to follow ME COME</u> - and these I shall counsel - these I shall lift up - and these I shall bless -- For I Am come that they might be found - sorted out and prepared - that they might enter into the Holy of Holies with Me ---

For it is now cone when many shall be brought out - and they shall be given a new body - a new place of abode - and they shall know that I AM - and that they have at last found their way into Mine Place of Abode -- I say it is the Way of the Initiate to WALK WITH SURETY ---

And as gentle as the fallen dew shall he go amongst them which know him not - for he - the Initiate shall not flount himself - neither shall he reveal himself unto the uninitiated -- For he shall be as silent as the sphinx -- He walks softly and silently amongst the unlearned - He hast at all times the authority and the power to assist the one which hast the WILL to follow Me -- He knows the true from the false -- So be it I speak into them which have ears to hear - and a mind to learn ---

SO BE it I AM

Sananda

Recorded oy Sister Thedra of the Emerald Cross

The Lord God vs "The Magician"

Beloved Ones -- There is a Plan - a time of fulfillment-- And the joy of that fulfillment no man knows -- So be it that I see the joy of its completion - for I see it as done -- And the time swiftly approaches when it shall be given unto thee to see as I see -- So be ye not anxious for that which is yet to come -- Wait upon Me - the Lord thy God -- Give unto Me credit for knowing that whcih I say unto thee -- Fear not for that which thou hast not yet seen - that which is to be -- Be ye blest this day and give into thineself Peace -- Let it be established within thee -- Be ye at Peace and Poise -- Seek not the fortune of the

108

magicians - for they are not of Mine Flock -- <u>For I give unto thee</u> <u>that which is sufficient unto thine salvation ---</u>

I say there are magicians which give unto them that which <u>they</u> <u>seek</u> -- Yet it is not the <u>ultimate</u> - it is not that which bringeth unto them Eternal freedom -- I Am come that thine <u>bondage</u> be <u>ended</u>! - <u>that thine ETERNAL FREEDOM be thine HIS DAY</u> -- <u>So be it I</u> <u>say: Follow ye Me</u> -- <u>Yet they weary of Mine Sayings</u> - and they turn unto the magicians that they might see his miracles! - that they might be given the miracles of flesh - the signs and wonders which doth astound them -- So be it that they are astounded by that which he does -- For this do they follow him - the wonder-maker - the magician ---

I say: I come not to astound them - neither to bewilder them -- I come that they might come into the FULLNESS of their Inheritance -- So be it I give unto them that which is sufficient unto their salvation -- Yet they have as yet not given unto ME credit for Being that which I AM ---

I say unto them which ask of Me: <u>Come! follow ye Me and I</u> <u>shall counsel thee - and I shall lead thee out of bondage FOREVER</u> -- So let it BE ---

For I come NOT preaching a strange or NEW DOCTRINE - I simply give unto thee the LAW which is as of old - that which shall be unto thee thine passport into the place wherein I Am -- I ask of thee nothing save obedience unto these and therein is thine own freedom -- So be ye as One self-responsible -- I Am come that it be SO ---

109

Recorded by Sister Thedra of the Emerald Cross

Their Strength Shall Fail Them

Beloved Ones -- This day let it be recorded that which I say unto thee -- The time draws nigh when the mighty hordes shall roam the streets as ones gone mad -- They shall pillage and burn the places wherein they have been -- As the offenders shall they be -- They shall be as ones obsessed -- And at no time shall they be given one iota of assistance from - or through the Mighty Council ---

These hordes shall strive to put down the law by which they have prospered - or by which they have benefited -- I say they are not respecters of the law - They shall give of themself that the law be put asunder - that it be broken -- And the pity or it - they too shall be broken! They too shall be put down - So be it that these are the ones which have not heard that which I say - These are not of a mind to follow after Me ---

I say unto thee - they have set into motion that which shall be their own undoing -- They shall be as ones gathered together - and as sticks they shall be broken - broken by twos and threes - yea by fours shall they be broken -- Yet there are the oppressors -- These too shall be broken as a reed upon a rock -- I say they shall see the frailty of their own strength in it shall fail them in that day - the day or Judgement -- Hear ye that which I say unto thee – it shall fail them in the Day of Judgement -- So be it I KNOW - yet I Am NOT the Judge -- I Am the One sent that there be LIGHT- So let it BE-- I AM

Recorded by Sister Thedra of the Emerald Cross

Light & Darkness

Beloved Ones -- Let this be given unto them which have ears to hear that which I say - for I say it that they too might know that I Am come for the good of ALL - for the GOOD OF ALL! ----

Let them too - know as thou knowest -- So be it that there is a movement abroad in the Lands of the Earth - to give unto <u>all</u> <u>men</u> freedom -- And this is not a small or insignificant thing -- Yet - I say man hast not the power to set them free - for the forces of darkness hast so woven their "web" that they - the people hast no power of their own -- For they have surrendered up their <u>will</u> -- They are possessed -- They are as ones filled with hatred --Now this is not of the forces of LIGHT -- I say: they have given of themself / their energy - unto the forces of darkness ---

Now it is coms when Great Light shall be upon ALL the peoples of the Earth - and there shall be great unrest - for the darkness shall be brought out of cover / uncovered - and they shall know wherein they have been bound ---

They shall see the folly of serving the forces of darkness -- They <u>shall</u> seek the Light - and IT shall not be denied them - <u>for when they turn from the darkness - they shall FACE the LIGHT</u> -- I say unto them which have wearied of the darkness - turn ye - follow ye Me and <u>I</u> shall LEAD thee into the Place wherein I abide - COME! and be ye free - even as I Am free ---

I Am the Lord thy God -

Sananda

Recorded by Sister Thedra of the Emerald Cross

Their Strength Shall Fail Them

Beloved Ones -- This day let it be recorded that which I say unto thee -- The time draws nigh when the mighty hordes shall roam the streets as ones gone mad -- They shall pillage and burn the places wherein they have been -- As the offenders shall they be -- They shall be as ones obsessed ---

And at no time shall they be given one iota of assistance from - or through the Mighty Council -- These hordes shall strive to put down the law by which they have prospered - or by which they have benefited -- I say they are not respecters of the law - They shall give of themself that the law be put asunder - that it be broken -- And the pity or it - they too shall be broken! They too shall be put down - So be it that these are the ones which have not heard that which I say - These are not of a mind to follow after Me ---

I say unto thee - they have set into motion that which shall be their own undoing -- They shall be as ones gathered together - and as sticks they shall be broken - broken by twos and threes - yea by fours shall they be broken -- Yet there are the oppressors -- These too shall be broken as a reed upon a rock -- <u>I say they shall see the frailty of their own strength in it shall fail them in that day - the day or Judgement -- Hear ye that which I say unto thee – it shall fail them in the</u>

Day of Judgement -- So be

it I KNOW - yet I Am NOT

the Judge -- I Am the One

sent that there be LIGHT-

So let it BE -- I AM

Sananda

Recorded by Sister Thedra of the Emerald Cross

Be Ye At Peace

Beloved Ones -- Be ye at Peace -- Peace I give unto thee -- Let thine time be Mine tine -- Rest in the knowing that I Am thine Shield and thine Buckler -- And at no time shall I deceive thee -- I hold thee within Mine embrace - and I shall not let thee go -- I Am cone that ye might have communion with Me - that ye might KNOW HE - that ye might be as ONE with Me -- I AM the ONE SENT that ye be found and brought out of bondage -- For long hast thou been bound in darkness -- Now ye shall wait upon Me the Lord thy God - and no other gods shall ye have before ME -- Such is Mine Word unto thee this day ---

So be it that I AM

Sananda

Recorded by Sister Thedra of the Emerald Cross

Signs of The Times

Beloved Ones -- The time arrives swiftly when there

shall be great black hordes roaming the streets - and

crying for blood -- For it is the fortune of them

which have been bound within flesh - to be as ones

bound - bound by the dragon - oppressed by him –

And they have held out their hand unto him - he hast

licked it - now he shall bite it - for he has no

scruples -- He hast no ethic -- He is the deceiver –

and the purveyor of lies -- He hast not the Grace of

the Lord thy God -- He is the one bound in perdition –

He hast not the will to let go the oppressed – He

hast the will to hold them bound -- <u>Now I say unto</u>

<u>thee - hold ye steadfast and turn not from the Light --</u>

<u>Fear not- and grovel not unto the ones which sit</u>

<u>in high places</u> --- <u>So be it I Am with thee unto the end</u> --

I AM Sananda

Recorded by Sister Thedra of the Emerald Cross

Aggressor / Oppressors / Pillage / Plunder

Beloved of Mine Being -- This is Mine time to speak out - for I Am silenced for long - and at no time shall I break Mine silence for naught -- I say it is NOW COME when I shall speak out against the <u>Aggressor</u> - against the ones which hold in bondage the oppressed - - I say these which hold in bondage the oppressed are the oppressors! - and they shall be as ones responsible for their own deeds of oppression and aggression!!---

I say that the aggression is that which hast been unto Me the stench in Mine nostrils -- For I say it is the aggression which is the downfall of many a nation and people -- They think to prosper by their aggression and pillage? - Nay Mine beloved NAY! ---

For a tine - they go forth to pillage / plunder / hold sway over the lesser nation - then they fall victim into their own weakness -- They fall into the pit which they have prepared for their brother ---

Let it be said that they which set the trap for their brother shall be bound therein -- I tell thee of a surety they shall not prosper! for it is the Will of The Father that ALL MEN be free -- Yet no man shall take upon himself the burden of another mans wrong doings - - He shall be as one responsible for his <u>own</u> actions / his deeds / his own "Sins"-- Let it be known NOW that each hast the responsibility of his own wrong doing - his own aggression -- And none shall find where the law justifies him for his aggression ---

I say unto them - be ye as the keepers of the law -- Take not the law into thine own hands - to thine own end - for thine own benefit!

I say it shall profit them not -- For that matter - it shall be their own undoing -- So be it I have spoken out - and I Am not finished - for I shall speak again and again - for that is Mine part - that the Way be made clear for the Ones which have asked of Me that they be delivered up - that they might have the opportunity to gain their own freedom from bondage -- Let them which have ears to hear - hear that which I say -- So be it - it shall profit them -- for this have I spoken ---

I AM the Lord thy God -

Sananda

Recorded by Sister Thedra of the Emerald Cross

Respect the Law

Beloved Ones -- It is now come when there shall be great rumblings within the Earth - as though the winds blow within Her -- There shall be great rumblings and groanings from within Her - and it shall cause great tidal waves - such as thou hast not known -- Yet I say it is given unto man to bring about his own downfall - for he hast not obeyed the Law - "LAW" - the Law set forth from the beginning -- I say the Law by which he shall live ere his deliverance from bondage ---

Now let it be said: I am not the Law Giver - I Am the <u>proclaimer</u> of the LAW - of which I speak -- <u>I Am the One sent that they might have the Law by which they SHALL LIVE ere they are delivered out</u> ---

116

So be it that they shall bring about their own downfall by their own disobedience unto it - their disrespect for the DIVINE LAW set forth by The Father Solen Aum Solen -- So be it I say unto them - LOOK! SEE! - Behold ye the HAND OF GOD -- See it MOVE - and be ye as ones awakened from thine lethargy -- I COME that ye awaken ---

I AM Sananda

Recorded by Sister Thedra of the Emerald Cross

The Household

Beloved ones -- While it is yet time for thine preparation - it is given unto thee to be as Ones with the vehicles of flesh - and for this do ye come under the law of flesh -- I say each hast its laws - laws for each and every place of abode - even as for each and every household -- Each a law - for each hast its "head" and each hast its feet -- Each hast a place within the whole of society -- "So above - So below" - for it is the GREATER household to which thou belongest -- It is Mine - and I Am the HEAD of this Household - and thou art Mine feet/ Mine hands / Mine Servants ---

So be ye as Ones prepared within the place wherein thou art - that ye might come into the Inner Temple with Me - and rejoice for thine preparation -- So be it I Am with thee - I AM NOT afar off -- So be it that I am the LORD THY GOD -

Sananda

Recorded by Sister Thedra of the Emerald Cross

117

Holy! Is The Name...

Holy! Holy! is the Name of Solen Aum Solen --

Speak It with reverence - and rememberance - for He

hast given unto thee LIFE - LIFE OF HIS LIFE --

And now it is thine time to remember that which

thou ART -- So be it I shall touch thee - and ye

shall remember -- So be it I AM the Lord thy God -

Sananda

Recorded by Sister Thedra of the Emerald Cross

Spirit Speaketh Unto Spirit

Beloved Ones -- While I say unto thee - the Spirit is that which motivates the flesh - that flesh comes under the law of flesh -- Yet the Spirit is free from the law of flesh - and the flesh is bound by the law of flesh-- While Spirit is not bound by any law of flesh nor Earth ---

The flesh is weak / perishable - while Spirit is imperishable - and cannot be contained in flesh ---

Spirit animates / uses / and holds for a time - and instrument of certain form / color / size / - releases it - and then takes upon itself another - and yet another - according unto its need / its desire / its likeness -- Wherein is it said: "From Glory unto Glory"?

118

Wherein is it said: "From the heights hast Spirit descended into the depth - and unto the heights shall it return - unscathed / unharmed for its descent" ---

Let it be known that Spirit speaketh unto Spirit - for flesh comprehendeth not that which Spirit sayeth---

So be it that I AM THAT I AM -

Sanand

Recorded by Sister Theara of the Emerald Cross

Spirit the Animator – Flesh the Manifestation

Beloved Ones: - This day let it be said that thine Mother Eternal hast nourished thee - and held thee unto Her Bosom - in the time of thine long sojourn within the realms of manifestation -- For it is by Me / for Mine part that thou hast been comforted / fed and nourished - while thou hast been within the manifested realms ---

While it is said - that "Ye shall return unto thine rightful estate" - I say ye shall no longer be bound in the denser world of the denser forms - the manifest world / that which is seen and felt by flesh---

Ye shall arise - and be free from that part which hast weighed so heavily upon thee -- So be it that I speak unto thee as thine Mother - for I AM THAT - and more - for I AM ONE with thine Father Solen Aum Solen - We are not TWO - WE ARE ONE - not divided / separate --

We are thine Eternal Parent - not ParentS ---

119

We are One with Our Creation - Our Manifestation - for thou hast come out of Mine womb - nursed at Mine Breast - YET NOT AS FLESH -- While it is given unto thee to have the parent of flesh - so dost thou have mother of Spirit -- For flesh is the counterfeit - or counterpart of Spirit - "So above - So below! " While the Spirit is but the Great Animator of flesh - flesh animates NOT -- Flesh is weak - and Spirit is free -- So be it that flesh comprehends NOT the things of SPIRIT ---

While Spirit KNOWS the weakness of flesh - It is the Animator - and the Greater --- In no way shall Spirit be less than SPIRIT -- And that which IS shall always BE -- While flesh shall pass unto is Source - that of the chemical world - the elements from which it is taken -- So be ye as Ones prepared to step forth as ones free from thine "pore" of chemical substance -- And be ye as ones free forevermore - as Ones GLORIFIED / free from bondage of flesh / of the manifest substance of the world of dense form ---

There are forms -- myriads of forms more glorious than thou hast imaged - which IS NOT of chemical substance - - Let the Mind which is Mine be the Mind which is thine - and I shall sustain thee - - I shall be unto thee ALL that thou hast need of - for I AM thine Mother Eternal -

Recorded by Sister Thedra of the Emerald Cross

The Age of Light

Beloved of My Being -- I say unto thee ye shall write that which I shall say unto thee and it shall be for the good of all mankind -- So be it and Selah ---

120

I say unto thee this MY WORD shall go out into thy home-land - and it shall be given unto them which are within that land and they shall be as ones prepared ---

For I say it is now come when there shall be great torment within that land ---

And it is given unto Me to know that which they shall encounter - and it is fortuned unto Me to be the one which has gone the long way that there may be PEACE upon the Earth -- Yet it is fortuned unto the ones which have been sent out from the den of the dragon - the forces of darkness - to be as ones which have the great determination to destroy themself ----

I say by their own doing shall they destroy themself!

Now it is within MY power to bring them out which have given of themself that there might be PEACE - yet it is given unto Me to know the Law concerning these things - and I say unto them - they which have sown into the whorl-wind - shall reap the whirl-wind -- So be it and Salah ---

Now ye shall say unto then in My Name that they which take up arms have already committed a guilt - and it is given unto Me to know that which I say unto them -- So be it and Selah ---

I say that they which give unto his neighbor the weapons or war has already committed a guilt - and he shall be as one held accountable for his own guilt - so be it the LAW -- Amen and Selah ---

Now say unto them as I would say - that they shall face portion which they have prepared for themself - and they shall eat thereof - and it shall be as gall in their mouth -- So be it and Selah ---

I AM come into the Earth that this may be the finish - that they which have the will to follow ME may be brot out ---

And I say unto thee - great shall be the sorrow and woe of them which betray themself -- So be it and Selah ---

I AM come into the Earth as One in a garment of flesh and bone - that The Father's Will may be done upon the Earth - and I shall not betray Myself - or the trust which has been placed Within Me - -

So be it that I AM within the Earth wherein sit many of My Brothers from the Higher Realms - and I say unto thee - We are sent of the Father that there may be PEACE ---

I say We bring not PEACE - yet We make way -- For PEACE shall be established upon the Earth - and She the Earth shall be cleansed - purified - and made new -- I say unto thee - it is the battle of Armageddon which is now come - for this battle shall be won within the realms of LIGHT - and the weapons shall be that of LOVE - PEACE and HARMONY - for these are the weapons of the wise - and the weapons which The Father has endowed unto US - Which HE has sent into the Earth at this time -- So be it and Selah - ---

I say unto thee - ye which have the mind to learn - and to comprehend - ye shall be as one alert - for One shall come unto thee in My Name - and He shall offer unto thee FREEDOM and PEACE which <u>no man</u> shall take from thee -- So be it in the Name of The Father - Son and Holy Ghost -- Amen ---

I Am the Son of God The Father - known within the Secret Place of My Abode as Sananda - once called Jesus - the Christ -- Amen - - So BE it ---

The War of Owai
Dec. 13, 1961

Beloved of My Being -- Ye shall now come to know what is meant by <u>a coward</u> and <u>a hero</u> - for there shall be one of each -- And one shall bear the skull and the cross bones - and the other shall bear <u>one banner</u> which has for its insignia the Crown and the Cross! I say unto thee - these two shall meet upon common ground and they shall come together as <u>one people</u> - yet they shall be divided -- And I say unto thee - they shall be as ones which serve God The FATHER - and HE shall not be mocked ---

So be it that HE shall make way for the Son of God The Father - which He has sent into the world at this time - Who now sits within the secret place of His abode - that The Father may manifest thru Him within the Earth ---

I say that the Son of God the Father - now sits in the secret place of His abode within the Earth - for the purpose of preparing some - which shall be brot into the place of His abode - which shall be prepared to go out - before He makes His <u>grand appearance</u> ---

And too I say that the day draweth nigh - when He shall go out from His secret place of His abode - with His <u>many</u> Emissaries

123

which now sit in council with Him -- And when the day dawns that They go out - there shall be a great laughing - and a great weeping - for therein shall be great joy - and a great wailing -- For them which know not the Son of God - shall fall down upon his face and cry for mercy -- So be it and Şelah ---

I AM HE which has been sent that this GREAT DAY may bear fruit - So shall it -- I say it shall bear new fruit - of a new variety - for the vine has been nourished - and the soil is now enriched from the LIVING WATER which has been brot from ON HIGH---

I say unto thee - that all which have come into the Earth as My Brothers of The Great White Star - are Ones which have received Their Inheritance in full - even as I have received Mine -- So be it that WE have come as thy BENEFACTORS - that even the lowly may receive their Inheritance in full -- So be it and Selah---

I AM Sananda - the Son of God The Father --

Amen and Selah --

Recorded by Sister Thedra of the Emerald Cross

Association of Sananda Sanat Kumara

"AS MESSENGERS OF THE CHRIST - IT IS OUR AIM TO ADD OUR "PORTION OF TRUTH TO ALL OTHER PORTIONS - BOTH ANCIENT AND MODERN - TO OTHER DIVINE WORDS OF GOD - THAT ALL MANKIND MAY BE DELIVERED FROM BONDAGE FOREVER ---

"THAT MANKIND MAY KNOW THE LAWS OF GOD - OUR FATHER - WHICH HAS GIVEN US OUR BEING IN THE BEGINNING ---

"THAT THEY MAY KNOW THE DAY OF DELIVERANCE HAS COME - THRU THE NEW DISPENSATION - AND THE RETURN OF THE LORD JESUS - THE CHRIST - NOW KNOWN AS SANANDA - AND HIS ASSOCIATES - KNOWN AS THE HOSTS OF LIGHT - THE PRINCELY CROWD - THE ROYAL ASSEMBLY - THE WHITE BROTHERHOOD - ETC ---

"TO PLACE BEFORE ALL PEOPLE EVRYWHERE - THESE 'PORTIONS OF THE HOLY SCRIPTURES' - UNADULTERATED - EV EN AS THEY HAVE BEEN ENTRUSTED UNTO US ---

"TO SURRENDER OUR WILL TO THE CREATOR - THE GIVER OF LIFE - THAT HIS WILL BE DONE IN US - THRU US - BY US - AND FOR ALL MANKIND"

From the School of Melchizedek

I - Thedra - have been entrusted with these words of our Benefactors -- our Sibors ---

The Lord Jesus Christ - known as Sananda by the Initiate - being the Director of the New Dispensation and at present upon the Earth in flesh and bone - has called me out from among "them" and has ordained me a Priestess in the Temple of Light - wherein He now sits in Council - and He has commanded me: "feed my sheep' -- And He has sent unto thee - this His servant - which He has ordained within His Secret Place - and given me the power and the authority to speak unto thee in His Name ---

And he has commanded that these WORDS - so entrusted into my keeping - be given as they were spoken - without one letter or one word being changed ---

I say with the authority which He has given unto me - it has been given unto me to go into the Place wherein He is - and sit within His Council Chambers - and now I say unto His sheep (the ones which have asked for LIGHT - and the ones who choose to follow Him) - that the Way is strait and the PATH is now made clear ---

Ye have but to read these WORDS with an open mind and a receptive heart -- And "fear not the pitfalls for they shall be marked well" - and you shall be given comprehension ---

Now the pages within this brochure are designed to bring you into the Place wherein He is - and I say with authority what you shall therein be prepared for greater things ---

My part is that of finding such Candidates for this initiation - and preparing them that they may receive yet another - and then they may be received within the Secret Place wherein He sits in Council - and therein the Initiate is given instruction for a "new part" and the PLAN shall be given unto him - and he shall be in accord with the great and grand PLAN of the New Dispensation -- He shall go out from the Secret Place prepared "as one wise" - as one which knows the LAW and he shall be as one with it -- So be it that he shall be as one which has the right to call himself Priest - or Priestess -- So be it in the Name of The Father - Son and Holy Ghost -- Amen and Selah -- Aum ---

Recorded by Sister Thedra

To you the reader of "The Sibors Portions", these words are addressed that you may know something about the one who has been and is the "Channel" thru whom these writings have been received. In the "Portions or "Holy Scripts", the messages are concluded by the words: "Recorded by Sister Thedra of the Emerald Cross" or "Recorded by Sister Thedra of the School of the Seven Rays". It should be self-evident that these titles could not and should not be used without proper authority.

To answer these and other questions that have been asked, we of the Association Sananda & Sanat Kumara, herein present a brief biographical sketch of Sister Thedra, that you might know something of the background of this remarkable woman; that you might come to know that it is only by the most intensive and extensive preparation, training, obedience, dedication and disciplines that one may become worthy to be used by such exalted Beings as Sananda (Jesus Christ), Sanat Kumara and other great Sibors and Teachers of the Higher Realms, to channel messages of Truth, Love and Hope to those who are Seekers of Truth", and who hunger for "The Bread and water of Life".

What is the background of Sister Thedra? What experiences did she need to go thru in order to become ready to be used as a channel? What are her qualifications and special Spiritual Gifts? What qualities of mind and character are required in order that one may ascend to that high position of responsibility that merits the recognition by our Blessed Lord God Sananda, as: "Mine Beloved", "Mine Beloved Priestess, whom I have authorized to speak in Mine Name"?

Sister Thedra - The Woman

The name 'Thedra" was given to her by the Lord God Sananda, at the beginning of her ministry. At an early age Sister Thedra manifested unusual ability to foresee events and facts by keen spiritual insight, or by what is now recognized as extra sensory perception. She was born in the year 1900. Educational facilities were limited in those days in her area, thus her education was somewhat limited.

She went thru many trials, frustrations and illnesses too numerous to mention, but it may be truly said that three on these illnesses literally took her thru the portals of death. It was only by the overshadowing protection of her blessed unseen Helpers, and by the power of her indomitable will, that she survived such severe illnesses as spinal meningitis, lymphatic cancer, partial paralysis, and a terrible automobile accident.

To elaborate somewhat on her third serious illness: In 1950 Sister Thedra was in an automobile accident, and was so severely injured that she was hospitalized and in a cast for 9 months, and was told by her doctors that she could never walk again - in fact they secretly admitted that they did not expect her to survive.

She was little more than a skeleton when the cast was finally removed, and she lay totally helpless, and could not move or help herself, and had to be carried and cared for like a baby. The day that the doctors removed the cast, they also discontinued all drug treatments. On this same day her earthly papa died, but they hesitated to tell her. The next morning when her doctor asked her: "Do I look like the bearer of news", she answered: "Yes I know - last night I walked with Papa part way, looking down on the earth.

As we went hand in hand, he turned to me saying: 'Honey you cannot go further, you must go back'". The doctor understood, for he had had a similar experience during the war. During her long months of agony in the cast, Sister Thedra had continual communication with Jesus, and was comforted by His assurances that He would be "with her all the way".

She came to the inner knowledge that she was actually and literally "In the palm of the Father's hand". It took nearly a year of the most determined, agonizing effort, which anyone of less determination would have given up as impossible, that this blessed one was able to finally get from her walker and wheel chair, on to crutches, for she had developed severe arthritis in her hips and hands.

By 1952 she was being subjected to treatments for lymphatic cancer in a clinic a great distance from her home. It was a torturous ordeal to prepare for the long trip (she was still struggling with her crutches) to the clinic for a series of treatments, even though her mother accompanied and assisted her.

When she was notified that it was time for another series of treatments, her very inner being rebelled - she felt that "There must be a better way". From the depths of her soul she cried out to the

Father: "Father Thy Will be done - if it is Thy Will heal me - if not I am ready to go". The One known to her then as Jesus appeared at her side and laid His hand on her throat, and she was instantly healed of the cancer.

He said that He would restore her to usefulness. She could have her complete healing now, or "Wait for the greater part". She replied at once: "I will wait for the greater part". She asked what she could do to repay such a debt; He answered: "Go feed My sheep - I will give you the Food and the Water".

Thru the powerful help of Sananda and her unseen Teachers, Thedra, by steel will and determination continued to improve, and was restored to usefulness, although she still had to struggle with her crippled body, and was never without pain. She was in continual communication with Sananda (then known to her as Jesus), and other great Teachers and Sibors, from whom she received revelations, prophecies and words of Living Truth, which she gave forth to the ever increasing numbers who sought her counsel.

During this time the One who has been known for centuries as Jesus revealed Himself to her in person, and gave her His New Name - Sananda, and instructed her to give it forth to all mankind.

The story of how Sister Thedra carried out His instructions; of how she carried on in the face of humiliations, tribulations and Judas type betrayals, when the forces of darkness seemed to be striving to disrupt and stop her work at any cost; of how, at the most crucial point of this trying time, Sananda's aides stepped in and whisked her away to a place of safety - never to return to her home again - would fill a volume! Some day, when the time is right, the full story of

Sister Thedra's life will be told, and it will be a thrilling story indeed!

After a few months in her "place of safety", Sister Thedra was instructed by Sananda to go to the region of Peru & Bolivia, in the high Andes mountains near Lake Titicaca. She was to go "without purse or script", and with only that which she could carry in her hand.

The following five years - from 1955 to 1961 - were spent under conditions of almost unbearable hardships, sacrifices, humiliations, privations, tribulations and severe discipline. She was instructed to get right down to bedrock, and live with and as the natives; to observe their hardships, filth, squalor and unbelievable poverty.

Thus she learned first-hand the lowly state in which people are fated to live very little better than animals. During this period of training and observation of the traits and habits of native existence, Sister Thedra learned the true meaning of Divine Love for these unfortunate people, who were experiencing the penalty meted out by "higher laws" to those who, in times past have betrayed their trust, and refused God's Grace when it was offered them - who chose the way of darkness. These were years of training her for the heavy responsibilities which, unknown to her, were to be placed upon her shoulders in succeeding years.

Few there are who could have faced the disappointments, humiliation and frustration she experienced when her inspired writings, received from Sananda and other Teachers and Sibors of the Higher Realms, were sent back to the United States at great personal sacrifice, often with postage taken from her very meager food money, only to be received with ridicule and scorn.

Many hundreds of pages of word for word recordings of the communications from these High Spiritual Beings were kept, and are to be found in the Holy Scripts which follow this "Portion". Among the great Beings who revealed themself and communicated with Sister Thedra during these years, was the great Angel Moroni, who foretold several years in advance, how He would arrange for a certain young man and young woman in the United States to meet and marry.

Moroni gave Sister Thedra many revelations and instructions which were to be delivered to the baby boy who would be born to this couple. This baby boy was to be the embodiment of Moroni, and was to be unlike any other child, in that he would be born with his memory - with his mind fully awake.

The story of how later, after Sister Thedra had returned to the states in 1961, the father and mother to be, as was foretold by Moroni, met and were married; and how the baby boy was born on the 24th of August 1963, is just one convincing proof of the accuracy and truth of the words "Recorded by Sister Thedra". The Temple Teachings contain many revelations and instructions which were given by Moroni to the parents during the pregnancy.

Intimate details are revealed regarding this remarkable child, and the part he is to play in history, and his destiny as a world leader. He will hold the fullness of the Melchezedek Priesthood, and will come in the office of one of the highest Angels.

How His coming is destined to affect every person, Church, Nation and people of the Earth, is only part of the mighty truths and disclosures of the "Work of the Father" – "The great and marvelous news" which have been "Recorded by Sister Thedra" - the humble and completely dedicated servant of God, who has been authorized by Sananda to "speak in His Name".